Robert Mushet

and the
Darkhill Ironworks

Robert Forester Mushet – the father of modern steel alloys.

Robert Mushet

and the
Darkhill Ironworks

'R. Mushet Special Steel goes on its way, single and alone, unapproached and although it has many would-be imitators, it has no competitors...'
The Railway Master Mechanic, *USA, February 1888*

Keith Webb

Black Dwarf Publications

THE

ROYAL FOREST OF DEAN

AND

HUNDRED OF SAINT BRIAVELS,

IN THE COUNTY OF GLOUCESTER.

Application for Registration.

To the Gaveller and Deputy-Gaveller of Dean Forest.

PURSUANT to an Act passed in the First and Second Year of the Reign of Her Majesty Queen VICTORIA, intituled, "An "Act for regulating the opening and working of Mines and "Quarries in the Forest of Dean and Hundred of Saint Briavels, "in the County of Gloucester," I *Robert Mushett* of *Coleford* do hereby declare that I was born at *Coleford* in the said Hundred of Saint Briavels, on the *Eighth* day of *April* in the year of our Lord *1812* and that I have worked a year and a day in a *Oak Wood Hill mine upper Level* within the said Hundred, that I am now abiding at *Coleford* within the said Hundred, ~~and following the trade or business of~~ and I hereby claim to be registered as a free Miner, pursuant to the provisions of the above-mentioned Act.

Name and residence of applicant to be here inserted in words at length.

Here describe whether a coal or iron mine, or a stone quarry, and also the particular mine or quarry.

As witness my hand this *Eighth* day of *September* 18 *38*.

Robert Mushett

Witness, *Wth: Mushet*
Traveller
London.

Robert Mushet's application for registration as a Free Miner.
8th September 1838.

CONTENTS

To June, my wife and friend
Her outstanding ability as a proof reader of my many drafts
improved the quality of my work beyond all recognition.
I am deeply indebted to her.

Copyright: Black Dwarf Publications and Keith Webb 2001

British Library Cataloguing-in-Publication Data. A catalogue
record for this book is available from the British Library
ISBN 1 903599 02 4

Black Dwarf Publications

47 – 49 High Street, Lydney, Gloucestershire GL15 5DD

www.blackdwarfpublications.co.uk

Printed by M.D. Jenkins Ltd.,
Unit 53/54, Lydney Trading Estate, Harbour Road, Lydney, Gloucestershire GL15 4EJ

Select Bibliography

The Bessemer Mushet Process or Manufacture of Cheap Steel. R.F. Mushet.
The Story of the Mushets. Fred M. Osborn. Thomas Nelson & Sons.
The Industrial History of Dean. Dr Cyril Hart. David & Charles.
Darkhill Ironworks and the Mushets. David Bick. Pound House.
Monuments Protection Programme. David Crossley. University of Sheffield.
The Severn & Wye Railway, Vol. 3. Ian Pope & Paul Karau. Wild Swan.
Man of Iron - Man of Steel, The Lives of David and Robert Mushet. Ralph
    Anstis. Albion House.
Historic Industrial Scene, Iron and Steel. W.K.V. Gale. Oxford University Press
The Victoria History of the County of Gloucester Vol. 5, The Forest of Dean.
    Ed. N.M. Herbert. Oxford University Press.
Southampton University Industrial Archaeology Group Journal No. 8 1999.
    Ed. Dr Edwin Course.

Keith Lloyd Webb BEM. JP.
is an Inclosure Commissioner for the Forest of Dean.

The first Commissioners were appointed in 1668 to ensure sufficient trees were planted, so that there was adequate wood to build the Navy's warships. Besides limiting the amount of Forest that can be enclosed, the Commissioners also ensure that areas which have previously been enclosed, are again thrown open to the public when the trees are big enough to continue growing, without further protection, to their maturity.

Introduction
and
Acknowledgements

When I first saw the ruins of Darkhill Ironworks at Gorsty Knoll, in the Royal Forest of Dean, I really fell for the place. Standing on the disused railway embankment, I saw before me the massive shoulders of a stone bastion rising above a sea of bracken. I felt as explorers must do when they first set eyes on the unknown, as I pushed my way through shoulder high fronds to get to the imposing stone walls and buttresses. That's when I fell. Unknowingly I had been walking towards a deep ravine that was cut by a small stream running through the site. Little did I know then the effect this was going to have on my life.

When we came to live at 'Marefold', we initially had little thought beyond our boundary walls capped with clinker-like lumps. That was until we were startled to find ourselves being watched by a large group of people beside the garden wall. Their tour leader was telling them that the stone for our boundary walls came from the nearby Ironworks.

Since then I have walked our dogs through the Ironworks and tried to pick up whatever might be gleaned from walls that stand as silent witnesses to what happened there. We became unofficial caretakers of the site and then I became a member of a small committee set up to look after Darkhill.

A day came when we gathered amidst the ruins and the Forest Enterprise representatives broke the news that they were going to have to enclose the site as they could be made liable for any injuries sustained by the public on the site. It had been fenced before but nature had removed all traces. I had been privileged to walk there without any feeling of restriction.

I felt physically sick as I accepted the implications of present day safety requirements. There was considerable protest from many quarters upon the site's enclosure. Generations of children had played on Darkhill without coming to any harm but I could not blame the authorities for having to protect the public from possible injury in the future. Suing anyone who might be blamed for accidents or injury has become common practice today.

Once Darkhill was fenced off I began to see that there were positive but unintended advantages. The damage caused by vandals has dropped to negligible proportions and the fencing does imply that here is a site of considerable importance. Having been involved, by implication, in the decision to enclose Darkhill I vowed that something positive must be done to replace the lost access.

This book may be a poor substitute for that vow but I hope it will increase our knowledge and understanding of Darkhill. Protecting the site is paramount if future generations are to have the opportunity to value what is left. We can not leave them to ask why we did nothing to protect Darkhill when we could.

Although I have written the text and taken many of the photographs, may I admit to not being an expert on the subject. I could not argue the analytical merits of one metal, or its production methods, over another.

Writing this text was a labour of love. I found the time needed because I thought it important enough to share what I had been told by others and also had been able to read on the subject. *The Story of the Mushets* by Fred Osborn (1952) and *Man of Iron - Man of Steel* by Ralph Anstis (1997) are but two sources. Robert Mushet's own published work (1883) takes us to the heart of the matter.

I have had some good tutors. Firstly Ian Standing, President of the Historical Metallurgical Society, who came and explained the meaning of the iron slag, clinker and other intriguing things that cap the boundary walls of my home, 'Marefold'. He infected me with his enthusiasm.

My second tutor has been Stan Coates, whose depth of knowledge on metallurgy and industrial archaeology is difficult to rival. While accompanying him, I have been privileged to listen to his meticulously chosen words as he has led many knowledgeable and distinguished parties around Darkhill.

My third tutor, friend, and mentor is Alec Pope. A highly respected and revered local historian, who would also claim he is not an expert. He has an inquiring mind and loves his Forest with every fibre of his body. He inspired the start and took part in the archaeological digs that took place at Darkhill in the mid 1960s and late 1970s. He has encouraged and coached me over the years.

He gave me the courage that culminates in the publication of this book. Our discussions and deliberations over the document, for very many months, has been the source of great joy to both of us.

Photographs are courtesy of June Webb, Donald Hicks, Peter Ellis, Alec Pope, John Dagley-Morris and Stan Coates, whose Darkhill collection of slides and files are in the safe keeping of the Dean Heritage Trust, along with a number of my own taking. Other photographs are courtesy of English Heritage, Trostre Works Cottage & Industrial Museum, Corus Packaging Plus and Moorland Publishing Company, whilst Nelson Thornes Ltd of Cheltenham graciously gave consent for photographs in Osborn's book to be reproduced. The staff at the Sheffield Industrial Museum Trust sites at Abbeydale Industrial Hamlet and Kelham Island Museum were very accommodating. Without the kindness and willing help of members of staff at The Dean Heritage Museum Trust at Camp Mill, Soudley, Forest of Dean much of this book would have been difficult to achieve. They have my heartfelt gratitude.

Thanks are also due to Ironbridge Gorge Museum Trust in Shropshire, Robert Guest, Deputy Surveyor of Forest Enterprise and the many residents of Gorsty Knoll.

Finally I should like to record my gratitude to David Hughes for his magnificent illustrations bringing the past back to life. He also redrew the Darkhill site plan, which is based on an original drawn up by Stan Coates and displayed at Darkhill by Forest Enterprises..

I hope I have done justice to the subject and been able to impart the knowledge that I have gained in an accessible and enjoyable manner. I feel my efforts would have been for nothing if my words had not been published by Neil Parkhouse of Black Dwarf Publications. I am also indebted to him for his encouragement.

Keith Lloyd Webb
Marefold
Gorsty Knoll
Forest of Dean
GL16 7LR
20 October 2001

Tump House, Cinder Hill, Coleford, the home of David and Robert Mushet. It is now the Forest House Hotel.

Robert Forester Mushet

Iron has been made since prehistoric times ('since time out of mind') but only in small amounts. Steel is an alloy of iron and carbon and it has better qualities for making weapons of war. There has always been an arms race and war has always motivated man's ingenuity more than almost anything else.

Steel had been made since the earliest days by repeatedly heating iron and beating out the impurities. It required skilled judgement of hand and eye. Overheating would affect the quality of the steel or make it useless.

All swords required hardening of the cutting edge to prolong their effectiveness. Some were made of iron with steel strips fused to the edge of the blade. Armour worn by knights and kings demanded other ingenious but laborious and costly methods of manufacture, requiring a lifetime's skills. The prize many sought during the 19th century was a method of making steel by cheap mass production.

Having replaced wooden ships with iron and then steel, the next major step forward was to find the vast quantities of thick armour plating needed to protect the battle ships of the early 20th century. Cannon balls had been replaced by shells. Then a metal suitable for making armour piercing shells was sought. Thus, technological progress leapfrogs on.

Without the capacity for large scale steel manufacture, history as we know it would have to be rewritten. Today steel is made by a continuous electric-arc furnace process, in quantities ranging from a tonne up to 200 tonnes at a time. The qualities and characteristics are easily changed for any required order.

The early days of commercial bulk production are a credit to the ingenuity of all involved. Some are, figuratively speaking, giants standing above all others, so great was their contribution in the march for progress. Confusion can arise from the terminology used both then and now. For example, the word 'furnace' does not have the same meaning today as it would have done then. The same applies to other technical terms.

The collapse of the coal mining and other traditional industries in the Forest of Dean, mainly for economic reasons and through no fault of their own, tore the 'heart' out of the Forest's people. When Fred Osborn was writing his authoritative book *Story of the*

Mushets in the late 1940s, many did not want to talk about the Mushets. In their eyes they were just another of the Forest's failures which they did not want discussed.

Some would put Robert Mushet forward as the first person to manufacture bulk steel and thereby challenge the importance of Henry Bessemer, the established father of mass production of steel making. Such arguments detract from both of their real importance in the world of steel making.

There is no doubt that Robert Mushet was way ahead of his time. Few of his contemporaries had the imagination to understand him and therefore most discounted him. Those who spotted the chance to make money invariably took advantage of him.

He must have been frustrated, impatient, and intolerant at times, as well as having constant worries about money problems. In fact, like many great men, he was probably his own worst enemy. He would get so embittered over the latest real or imagined snub that some, who could have been of help, attacked him in print instead.

Robert was born at Tump House, Coleford on April 8th 1811, eight years before Queen Victoria was born. He was the last of seven children in the family and was baptised on 23rd July 1812. In those days, it was unusual to delay baptism for so long after birth, as child mortality was high and Robert was a sickly child. Babies were thus baptised as quickly as possible, so that in case of an early death they could at least be given a Christian burial, which was of great importance and comfort to the bereaved.

He was not baptised with the middle name of 'Forester' but he used it, in later years, to drive home the point that he was born and bred in the Forest of Dean. Anyone, who was not, was looked upon as a 'foreigner'. Robert was justly proud of being a Forester.

He went to Cambridge University but his studies were curtailed by poor health and he returned to the Forest to help his father run his Darkhill Ironworks on Gorsty Knoll, to the south-east of Coleford. He later became a Free Miner, as he was entitled to do having been born within the Hundred of Saint Briavels.

He also had to have worked in a mine for a year and a day to qualify. This he did in his father's mines and he was well thought of by other workers for having gained his status by hard work. Agnes, his mother, claimed that he was the first 'Gentleman' to do so. There had been others, of course, but this reflects the pride of mothers the world over.

Forest House Hotel, as Tump House is now known, is situated beside the Forest of Dean District Council Offices, in the centre of Coleford. It was leased by Robert's father, David Mushet. When his father retired and went to live in Monmouth, Robert and his family moved into the house. A blue and white plaque beside the front doorway proclaims it as having been the residence of the Mushets.

Robert married Mary Ann Thomas, from St Briavels, in 1841. They initially lived at Edenwall House, in nearby Coalway. The first of their three children, Tom, was born there a year later, followed by Henry in 1845. They then moved to Tump House, where their youngest child, Mary, was born in 1850.

Robert was described as being tall and shy. He could easily get upset over whatever he considered an injustice and it was claimed that he had outgrown his strength during his adolescence. Although he was happily married, he was dogged by ill health. Unfortunately, his doctor described him as being a victim of incurable hypocardiosis, which might mean he did not know what was wrong or that Robert thought he suffered from everything conceivable.

It is said that Robert was driven by nervous energy and frequently burnt himself out by overwork on his father's affairs. Robert gained valuable experience in iron making from his father but it was becoming apparent that he was also a gifted metallurgist in his own right.

There was considerable friction with his brothers who had ideas other than iron making. He felt all the worry fell on him. The domestic problems within the family would have broken the spirit of a lesser man. Although the youngest of the three sons, he became manager of the Darkhill Works in November 1845. The constant quarrelling between the brothers had unfortunate consequences in the daily running of the ironworks.

The eldest brother had artistic aspirations and had no interest in working at Darkhill. The middle brother also had ideas of his own but was only interested in the works for what money he could make out of it for his own schemes. Working practices were chaotic. Water often ran into the molten iron, exploding on contact with disastrous results. There are stories of workers running about with their clothes on fire. The area would not only have been heavy with smoke from the works but 'blue' with language too! A year after the death of their father, Darkhill Ironworks was put up for auction but remained unsold.

Robert Mushet took out fifty-four patents on his work but he had neither the income nor the commercial acumen to protect his interests. At a crucial time, his business partners did not pay, as they had promised, the £50 stamp duty due on his patents in their third year, and thus it became a free-for-all. He was let down like this many times.

Steel for the first steel railway rails was made by Robert Mushet. The double-headed rail was rolled at the Ebbw Vale Iron Company's works, where he had connections. In 1857 the rail was laid at Derby, between the station and the locomotive sheds, where the Midland Railway had been experiencing problems with the iron rails they used, which needed replacing every three to five months.

For ten years the new rail showed no signs of wear, although some two hundred railway vehicles a day passed over it. Because of its historic importance Robert made repeated requests to have it returned to him when it was no longer useable. It was scrapped in 1873, only months prior to his last request. He described it as an act of vandalism on the part of the Midland Railway. He claimed that during its life more than 1,252,000 locomotives and tenders had safely passed over it.

When he developed self-hardening steel, in 1868, for the manufacture of mining drills and other uses where heat would affect the performance of the steel, he took the decision not to patent the process but to keep it a secret.

It is regrettable that there was ever any antagonism between Robert Mushet and Henry Bessemer but both had their point of view. Robert, like his father, would frequently fire off a letter to the press to correct what he thought was a slight or because he felt he was not getting the credit that was his due. There were many battles of words in the press as he confronted his critics. There were years of controversy, echoes of which still reverberate even today.

In later years, they were reconciled and both paid the other generous tributes but only the conflict is remembered – controversy makes for a much better story. As time passed, the Mushets became virtually unknown, whereas Bessemer went on to worldwide fame and fortune, and became a household name.

In 1876, the 'Bessemer Gold Medal' was awarded to Robert Mushet by The Iron and Steel Institute, their highest award. The citation referred to the role of father and son in ferrous metallurgy and specifically to Robert's invention of the Spiegeleisen process for bulk steel making. He was only the third person to receive the award. Unfortunately, the die was cast. Robert Mushet was ill again and therefore he was not present to receive the medal or to hear Bessemer's public tribute to him.

Subsequently, Robert admitted, *"I had merely supplied the rudder, as it were, to the Bessemer ship, and a rudder is indispensable no matter how otherwise complete the ship may be, and in this instance it was truly a magnificent barque... all but the rudder!"* Later, he less diplomatically wrote, *'Bessemer metal without Mushet = IRON: Bessemer metal with Mushet = STEEL".* Not a strictly accurate statement but its brevity still made his point.

The secret of the 'R. MUSHET SPECIAL STEEL' (self-hardening steel) ingredients was passed to his son Henry, who went to work for Samuel Osborn in Sheffield. Extraordinarily, the secret was kept until it was published some eighty years later.

A lesser known claim to fame was the Dozzle, designed and made by Robert. It was fitted into the top of ingot moulds, to retard cooling and reduce the amount of metal which had to be rejected, because a shrinkage pipe would form after the molten metal cooled. Robert's method of using china clay in the manufacture of crucibles increased the amount they would hold and doubled the number that could be used at any one time. Output and profits were thereby greatly increased.

He had kept this method secret too, for some years, until (so he claimed) two of his workers betrayed him. Robert claimed to have saved Sheffield steel makers many millions of pounds and felt he had been taken advantage of whilst not receiving the slightest acknowledgement for the benefit of his inventions.

Robert wrote a small volume entitled *The Bessemer – Mushet Process or the Manufacture of Cheap Steel* in 1883. In it he wrote, *"I owe nothing to the world; but the world is largely indebted to Sir Henry Bessemer and to myself. I owe nothing to any steelmaker for my knowledge, such as it is. I was never inside any steelworks but my own. I have no special talent to boast of; but I had perseverance and inflexible determination, which have given me a measure of success, and I am told my steel is preferred, though at a higher price, to any other steel manufactured at home or abroad.*

I fear many who may deem my book worthy of a perusal will consider me as egotistical and self-asserting; but with the object I had in view, I could scarcely, consistently, write otherwise."

Another view of Tump House, the family home of the Mushets. Since the picture was taken, this Grade II listed building has been sympathetically restored. Whilst the fabric of the building was exposed, the author took the opportunity to look at the many structural changes which had been made throughout the building's life.

The outbuildings at Tump House, where both David Mushet and his son Robert carried out many of their experiments. The buildings were demolished in the early 1960s. Houses now stand in their place but there is a plaque on a nearby wall recording their existence.

Some of the remaining buildings of the Titanic Steelworks. Since this picture was taken, the roof of the stables on the left has collapsed.

Milkwall Brickworks, which lay between the Darkhill Ironworks and the Titanic Steelworks. All that remains today are some mounds hidden in the grass and bracken. There is a brick kiln on the right. The Sling – Fetterhill road runs behind the buildings and Ellwood is on the skyline. The buildings were no doubt built by the Mushets when the upper terrace of Darkhill Brickworks was abandoned for that purpose.

A view of the Titanic Works buildings from the railway line, prior to their demolition in the early 1960s.

A view of Gorsty Knoll about 1910. The remains of Darkhill Ironworks appear on the right, whilst the equally derelict Titanic Steelworks can be discerned in the left distance, just above the trees. On the skyline above that is the chimney of Easter Iron Mine. Just beyond the railway is Aaron's Pond, which mistakenly appears on some maps as Heron's Pond. Aaron Hart had a licence to water his horses here around 1900. The pond was formed when the railway embankment was built in 1874 and it supplied water to the Titanic Works. At the bottom of the slag heap bank was a small pump house supplying a pond beside the Milkwall Brickworks and the Titanic Works.

There was no greater accolade for Robert Mushet than that written in *The Railway Master Mechanic*, published in Chicago in February 1888: '*R. Mushet Special Steel goes on its way, single and alone, unapproached and although it has many would-be imitators, it has no competitors, and appears to be as little likely to be duplicated as the celebrated Damascus blades are likely to be. Good steel is made in this (USA) country . . . As good perhaps as can be found anywhere . . . but the Mushet fills a niche in a way that none other can.*'

Although undoubtedly gifted, he worked in some isolation, and therefore was not always aware of what was already in the public domain, whether in literature, patents or practice. He did things the hard way and at times 're-invented the wheel' without realising it. But for all that he was an original thinker and resolved many of the problems that beset the steel industry at a critical time in its history. We readily forget there was not the advantage of instant electronic communication that we have today.

Throughout the rest of his life, he felt deeply aggrieved and hurt at having been 'wronged'. It may have been this resentment which drove him on to his greatest achievement, one which dwarfed everything else he did, This was the discovery of self-hardening steel, what we know of today as machine tool steel. He was the first to experiment with manganese, tungsten, titanium and chrome in the successful making of steel alloys. These were breathtaking and far sighted achievements.

With so much on his mind he overlooked that the lease on Tump House, taken out by his father, had unfortunately expired. To make matters worse, his brother-in-law, the Rev. George Roberts, married to Robert Mushet's sister Henrietta, was trying to get him evicted. In addition, George Roberts disputed Robert Mushet's execution of David Mushet's estate. The Mushet family thought it a poor return for having helped the Rev. Roberts financially through university.

By October 1866, his accusers were writing to him at Belgrave House in Cheltenham. Even so he still intensified his experiments at Darkhill, whilst overseeing the building of the Titanic Works and subsequently taking on its management over the following years. A lesser man would not have achieved as much as he did in such circumstances. He died on 29th January 1891. His old friend Samuel Osborn, by then Mayor of Sheffield, and his son, Samuel Osborn junior (by then Sir Samuel Osborn) attended the funeral in Cheltenham.

David Mushet

David Mushet

Children learn a great deal from their parents so our story has to include a little about Robert's father, from whom he inherited his interests in the manufacture of metals. It was David Mushet who had built Darkhill Ironworks in 1818.

Originally from Scotland, he was a brilliant metallurgist. He came to Coleford for the express purpose of making the Whitecliff Furnace, to the south-west of Coleford, a success but, after the loss of the fortunes of those involved, he started his own ironworks at Darkhill. He made iron there for 20 years.

During those years he perfected the making of superior quality refined iron, which was more malleable and suitable for tinplate making by direct smelting. Modern technology has only proved capable of achieving this process in recent years.

In 1845, David conveyed the works to his three sons who were always quarrelling. Each brother blamed the incompetence of the others when things went wrong. Consequently, and no doubt behind their ailing father's back, the brothers attempted to sell the works and collieries by auction. The auction particulars provide invaluable details of these concerns and are included here in full:

FOREST OF DEAN, GLOUCESTERSHIRE

Blast Furnace and Collieries.
TO BE SOLD BY AUCTION,
BY MR. WHITE,

At the BELL INN, in the City of GLOUCESTER, on TUESDAY, the 13th day of JULY, 1847 at three o'clock in the afternoon punctually,

IN ONE LOT,

THE newly erected and valuable BLAST FURNACE for the smelting of Iron, called

"Dark Hill Furnace,"

with the engines, machinery, apparatus, hot blast stoves, casting house, carpenters' and blacksmiths' shops, and other buildings, coke-yard, furnace-yard, water ponds, reservoirs, lands and appurtenances thereto belonging and adjoining, the site whereof comprises in the whole

5A.3R.17P. or thereabouts, situate within a few yards of the Severn and Wye Railway, and of the turnpike road leading from Coleford to Park End and Blakeney in the township of West Dean, in the Forest of Dean.

ALSO, the two very desirable COAL MINES, GALES or LEVELS of COAL, called

Dark Hill & Shutcastle Collieries,

adjoining each other, situate in the said township of West Dean, with the buildings, coke-yards, tram plates, and other matters and things used in working the same collieries, and now being in, upon, or under the same.

The Collieries comprise the coal under about 100 acres of land, and are estimated to contain 6000 tons per acre of the Coleford High Delf Coal in a vein of 6 feet thickness.

The mouth of the Dark Hill Level lies within 50 yards of the Severn and Wye Railway, and within about 300 yards of the Furnace.

The Blast Furnace is capable of making from 50 to 70 tons per week of Pig Iron which can be manufactured and delivered at the shipping port of Lydney for a cost, including every expense, not exceeding 55s. per ton.

THE DARK HILL COLLIERY is subject to a yearly rent or Royalty of three half-pence for every ton of Coal brought out, payable to the Crown half yearly, and if such rent shall not amount within any year to £3, then a rent of £3 in lieu thereof.

THE SHUTCASTLE COLLIERY is subject to a yearly rent or Royalty of one penny for every ton of Coal brought out, also payable to the Crown half-yearly, and if such rent shall not amount within any year to £2, then a rent of £2 in lieu thereof.

Two undivided third parts or shares in the Blast Furnace and Lands and Collieries are *freehold of inheritance. The other one undivided third part* is held by lease for the remainder of a *term* of 21 years (except the last three days of the said term) commencing on the 1st day of January, 1846, and is subject to the payment, to the Proprietor of such one-third part, of 3s.4d. for every ton of Pig Iron made upon the premises, and 3d. for every ton of saleable Coal raised or gotten out of the premises, other than and except the coal fairly raised for household purposes by workmen employed in the said Mines and Works, and other than and except any coal consumed in the making or manufacturing Iron upon the said premises ; but if the said rent of 3s. 4d. per ton of Pig Iron shall not amount in any half-year to £100

then the sum of £100 is to be paid in lieu thereof for
such half-year.

An abundant supply of excellent **IRON MINE**
can be obtained at a price ranging from 5s. to 7s. per ton
delivered at the Furnace-yard; and Fire Bricks are made
in a Brick yard adjoining the property.

Further particulars and information respecting the pro-
perty may be obtained of ROBERT MUSHET, Esquire,
Coleford, Gloucestershire; or of Messrs. POWLES,
TYLER, & POWLES, Solicitors, Monmouth.

There were either no takers or, which seems more likely, the
properties were withdrawn from the auction before it went ahead.
It is difficult to believe that these desirable concerns would not
otherwise have found a buyer. Possibly the whole idea was part of
the financial manoeuvrings between the three Mushet brothers, or
perhaps Robert thought it may have been a way of him gaining
sole control.

David Mushet died on the 7th June 1847. In his last years he
lived in Monmouth and he is buried in Staunton churchyard.
During his life, he had repeatedly complained that he was a poor
man. He risked going to Debtors Prison for refusing to pay money
he owed, his friends paying the debts at the last moment to prevent
such actions being carried out. He had constantly complained that
his sons thought he had money to waste on them. As a result, it
came as a shock to find that he had died a wealthy man.

Henry Bessemer as a young man. A pencil drawing by John Pottinger.

Henry Bessemer

Henry Bessemer was born on 19th January 1813 at Chalton, in Hertfordshire, the son of an engineer. During his lifetime he altered the course of history by some of his inventions, which met the needs of war and the demands of commerce.

He is the recognised father of bulk commercial steel making and no-one should take away the credit that is due to him. He was financially independent, an engineer, and entrepreneurial inventor. He was not an Ironmaster and that was held against him. He was seen as an upstart by many Ironmasters, who had long histories of experience to justify their standing. He was resented and had a hard time making his place in history but he ruthlessly suppressed all those whom he thought were taking away the credit due him.

To understand the controversy over who can be credited with the making of the first mass-produced steel, it is necessary to understand who did what, when and the parts played by Robert Mushet and Henry Bessemer. Bessemer claimed to have made the first steel rails, laid in Crewe station on the London & North Western Railway in 1863, which was seven years after Robert Mushet had his laid in Derby Station.

Mushet's rail may have been a one-off but it was still a first of its kind and the method of production was sound. Bessemer developed the commercial exploitation of mass steel production.

Since the early problems have been overcome, steel has been made all over the world using the Bessemer Converter method. Unfortunately, he licensed Ironmasters to make steel by his new method before the whole process was fully understood. Allegations of fraud were made, not to mention threats, when the process did not work. This was when the iron ore used contained impurities such as sulphur or phosphorus, there being no understanding at that time of the effect they would have.

Bessemer had jeopardised his whole fortune in trying to make his invention work. As everything went wrong, he heard that steel was being successfully made in the Forest of Dean without these problems. In desperation he hurried to Coleford and tried to see Robert Mushet several times but to no avail.

Mushet was correcting the balance for making steel by adding a measured amount of spiegeleisen, a natural ore from Germany that contains iron, carbon and a small amount of manganese, which would completely remove any sulphur present. This process also put back the right amount of carbon, about 1%, to make high quality steel. The other impurities were being trapped in the slag.

On calling yet again at Tump House, Bessemer was inadvertently told by a nervous servant, who was somewhat overwhelmed by Bessemer's forceful nature, that Mushet really was out somewhere in the town and that it was not a case of being 'not at home' to an unwanted guest.

Bessemer went looking for him. Mushet, however, must have spotted him and avoided him by hiding behind his umbrella as they passed each other. One would have imagined that the incident occurred somewhere near the Angel Hotel, where Bessemer might have stayed.

It is a frozen moment in time that should be immortalised in the centre of Coleford town by a sculptured tableau of two distinctively dressed Victorian figures passing one another, with one hiding behind an umbrella. It would help to raise the awareness of the importance of Robert Mushet in the town's history.

Iron ore from the Forest of Dean was low in sulphur content, unlike iron from other parts of the country. Therefore, there were fewer problems in smelting Forest ore but it was not easily mined. When Bessemer's process was finally made to work, the Forest's iron lost its unique position. Vast quantities of iron ore, mined easily using opencast methods, could be used for making steel even more cheaply instead, despite its sulphur content.

Unfortunately, Robert remained loyal to the Ironmasters in South Wales with whom he had worked, although he was let down by many of them as they dashed to make their fortunes from the Bessemer process of manufacturing cheap steel, in bulk.

By 1866 Robert Mushet was in ill health again and destitute. His 16 year-old daughter, Mary, was distressed seeing the way her father was being treated by those she thought he had helped. She took her courage in both hands and travelled to London with grim determination.

This was quite an undertaking when seen against the background of the difficulties of travel, and the customs and etiquette of her day. The reason given for her trip was that she was going to visit her uncle who worked in the Royal Mint, which in those days was situated in the Tower of London.

Instead, she confronted Bessemer in his office. One of his clerks announced the visit of a young lady, who would not send in her name but wished to see him personally. Not the done thing in those days. Even so, she was invited into his private office. Although dressed in her best clothes, for her visit to London, she would have been looked upon as a child from the provinces and therefore any social impropriety might have been overlooked. When face to face she told him her name and said she understood that Mr Bessemer's success was based on the results of her father's discoveries.

She made it clear to him that although her father might not have any legal claim upon Bessemer she felt he had a justifiable moral one. When Bessemer asked how much her father owed she held out a piece of paper she had been clutching tightly in her hand, with the details. Without hesitation, Bessemer wrote her a cheque for £377 14s. 10d. to cover her father's debts, a considerable sum of money in those days. She thanked him in a faltering voice and he bid her a curt *"Good afternoon"*.

This sum covered her father's debts and thus safeguarded her parents from losing their home. Bessemer's business partner was alarmed when he heard what he had done. He accused him of being imprudent but when he understood that it had come out of Bessemer's own private account he was mollified. Bessemer subsequently made Robert Mushet an annual allowance of £300 (equivalent to £20,000 today), explaining he did so to make Mushet his debtor, rather than the reverse.

Henry Bessemer was knighted in 1879. At the time a letter appeared in *The Times* which stated that a similar honour ought to have been bestowed on Robert Forester Mushet.

Described by contemporaries as a proud and assertive man, he may have had a kinder heart than he wished to be generally known. Robert's wife, Mary, continued to receive half her husband's pension from Bessemer's estate until she died, at the age of 96, in the spring of 1914. Robert's pension could easily have lapsed upon his death and Bessemer had died in 1898.

Converter in volcanic action at the Workington Works, Cumbria, in 1974.

The Bessemer Converter

Initially, there were many teething problems because this aspect of the science of steel making was in its infancy. The effects that impurities had were not understood and also where they came from was still not recognised. Cast iron from a blast furnace has a high carbon content, which makes it brittle.

To make good steel, a small amount of carbon is essential. The impurities in iron have either to be removed or their quantities controlled. The molten iron from the blast furnace is charged into the top of the converter, whilst it is horizontal. The converter is raised into an upright position and air is blown through the charge.

With the converter, impurities such as sulphur, phosphorus and silicon were either trapped in the slag, burnt off by blowing air through the molten iron, or absorbed in the converter's added special lining. The skill was in the eye of the Melter, who had to judge when the moment was right to stop the process. He watched

The last converter used in Britain in 1974 which worked on Bessemer's principles. It came from the Workington Ironworks, Cumbria of the then British Steel Corporation (now Corus). It was presented to the Kelham Island Museum, Sheffield in 1978 and stands outside the museum's main entrance.

One of the three 25 ton converters at Ebbw Vale 'blowing' in the 1950s. The one on the left is turned down ready and waiting for its charge of scrap metal and hot molten iron.

the change of colour and the type of sparks rocketing out of the top of the converter. It would then be poured and cast into ingots.

Bessemer's own description of his converter in action was as "*a veritable volcano in a state of active eruption*". Temperatures of 1,650 degrees Centigrade or 3,000 degrees Fahrenheit were achieved in the process. By chemical reactions, the iron is converted to steel. It took about 20 minutes for a 25 ton charging.

Although Bessemer had proposed and patented the use of oxygen in his converter as far back as 1856, bulk supplies were not available and they had to use air, which, because it is part nitrogen, causes its own problem. When 20th century technology caught up with him and oxygen could be mass-produced, the Bessemer converter method became even more efficient.

The Darkhill Ironworks

If visiting the Darkhill Ironworks site by car, park in Forest Enterprise's car park on the Sling/Fetterhill/Parkend Road south of the crossroad with the Milkwall/Ellwood Road. A short track from the car park leads to a cycleway on the bed of the old Severn & Wye Railway branchline from Parkend to Coleford. Turn right for the best overall view of the ironworks. It is also possible to walk round its perimeter.

Where you join the cycleway, from the car park, is known locally as 'The White Gates', because there were once gates here to allow horse drawn traffic to cross the railway to reach Titanic Steelworks and the Milkwall Brickworks.

On a sunny day, it is easy to walk to the ironworks from the centre of Coleford. It is a pleasant stroll along the cycleway on the disused railway line and many people use it to walk the mile and a half to Darkhill and back.

The branchline, authorised by an Act of Parliament of July 1872, was opened to goods traffic in July 1875 and to passenger trains five months later. The curvature of the line at Darkhill was so severe it required a checkrail for safety. Trains would be moving at a walking pace, caused by a combination of the gradient, curvature and checkrail. It was a difficult branch line to work and maintain.

The engine house of the Easter Iron Mine can be seen from the cycle track at Milkwall. Robert Mushet leased the mine in May 1846 to supply his undertaking with iron ore. The edge of the coal measure arises on Gorsty Knoll, reached easily by drift mining (tunnelling into the hillside).

The Darkhill Ironworks are on the southern-most slope of Gorsty Knoll. As you come to the site of what might be mistaken as an Inca ruin you find, beside the road, on the left of the cycleway, stands the crossover of a railway line point, mounted upright, on a plinth.

The monument raised in 1999 is an eye-catching tribute to the work of David Mushet and his youngest son Robert. It is hoped that it will capture the imagination of visitors and make them want to explore the area, and go on to learn more about the importance of what went on here and its impact on our world of today.

A metal plaque on the stone base proclaims a simple message:

> David Mushet 1772-1847 and son
> Robert Forester Mushet 1811-1891.
>
> **Outstanding Metallurgists.**
>
> In this valley early experiments in the making
> of STEEL and its alloys were carried out.
>
> **Thus the Age of STEEL began.**
>
> Forest Enterprise   Forest of Dean Local History Society

David Mushet's efforts contributed much to the advancement of making iron direct from a furnace. Robert Mushet's pioneering work helped find the answers to the bulk production of cheap steel. The key to unlocking the door to consistent quality in the bulk production of steel was finding a reliable way of getting rid of the impurities in the molten metal and controlling its carbon content. Robert's even greater achievement was to carry out some of the first experiments in the production of steel alloys.

Looking down on the site from an observation area beside the cycleway, there is only a general idea of how the complex was used in Robert Mushet's day because of the subsequent use to which the buildings were put. Further down at the lowest level in front of the tall arch, lying beneath a protective layer of soil, is a 'horseshoe' shaped hearth that was never fired. It poses the question, did Robert alter key structures so that anyone buying the site could never learn anything of value?

It makes a good but groundless story even though items have been removed and one has been hidden some distance away. To add to any confusion or sense of mystery, in modern times, a nearby arch has been altered to an angular one at the whim of a 'restorer'. Other clues have been lost during restoration repairs.

Iron ore and other materials would be barrowed out from the building on the middle level, directly above the tall archway, via a charging bridge. The remains of the stone causeway can be seen. The last few metres to the top of the retort may have been a metal walkway, which would have later been taken for scrap.

There is insufficient water here to turn a waterwheel for a bellows. A steam engine must have been planned from the start for the power needed. There were two ponds, at the lower end of the site, that would have supplied the engine. The present pond was formed much later by the building of the railway embankment.

To the right of the tall arch is the ideal location for a steam-powered, beam operated, blowing engine for the furnace. There is some good evidence that it was situated here. After this part of the site was abandoned, much of the stonework was robbed. When the engine was removed, part of the building may have been knocked down to get it out. It is said that some of nearby Milkwall is built of stone from here.

Present day specialists in iron and early steel making, visiting the site of the Darkhill Ironworks, are unable to conclude what precisely went on here, partly because the buildings have been altered but also because it was a period of rapid development. Because many of the alterations were of a temporary nature, savings were made by altering or making do with items already there.

Some distance away there is a pile of large, moss covered boulders. Amongst them is a large mass of a different texture. It is a 'Bear', lying on its side, half-hidden by the stones. A 'Bear', in metal smelting terms, is a solidified mass of impurities, scum that had been skimmed off before the molten metal was tapped. The 'Bear' had been hidden until some of the stones, with time, rolled down the slope. Why had so much physical effort been used to bring so many tons so far. Was Robert Mushet trying to hide a secret?

Tramroads ('dramroads' locally) were the forerunner of railways. Horse drawn wooden wagons, with flangeless wheels, ran along 'L' shaped cast iron rails, which faced outwards. The rails enabled heavier loads to be hauled than was possible on the rutted roads of the time. David Mushet put up money, in partnership with others, to build this branch to Milkwall in 1812. The traffic, initially, would have been stone from the nearby quarries and felled timber from the Forest. When Darkhill came into production, iron ingots would have made their way down to the tin works at Parkend and beyond.

As the path widens above where the 'Bear' is located, there were two tracks. Some tramroad blocks can be seen but most are hidden beneath years of rotted leaf mould. One of the tracks was a loop. The stone blocks forming this line have only one hole in their centre. These date from the earliest days of tramroad building. The rail was held by a spike driven into an oak peg in the hole.

Most of the stones that make up the more heavily used 'running line' beside the loop have either two or three holes in them. Single-spike stones were found inadequate with heavy usage, so a 'chair' was adopted for holding the rail, requiring two holes. The blocks with three holes are original single-holed stones which were modified to take a chair. The twin-holed blocks are later replacements.

Some tramroad stone sets cross the track at an angle. When not hidden by bracken a tramroad profile can be seen leading off down a slope towards the works. This was laid in 1818 to serve the middle level of the works. A later spoil tip from a drift coalmine has obliterated some of the route.

Almost hidden there is a spring, beside the path that runs down by the works from the tramroad. This spring looks insignificant today but it was of vital importance to the people who lived and worked here in the past. It took on an historic significance beyond its size when a dispute arose about it in 1866 between the Crown and Mushet:

> AN INDENTURE made the seventeenth day of October 1866 between the Queen's Most Excellent Majesty of the first part, the Honourable James Kenneth Howard, the Commissioner for Her Majesty's Woods and Land Revenues to whom the management of the Royal Forest of Dean has been assigned of the second part, and Robert Mushet of Belgrave House, Cheltenham in the County of Gloucester, Iron Master, and Goodrich Langham of Coleford in the County of Gloucester of the third part ... these two gentlemen claim to be proprietors of certain premises and buildings now used as a smith's shop, situated at Dark Hill in Parkend or York Walk, and that at some time they laid down certain pipes for the purpose of conveying water to the said smith's shop, under certain wastelands of the said forest, without any license or authority from Her Majesty or Commissioner ...'.

> The Indenture then 'calls upon and requests the said Robert Mushet and Goodrich Langham to accept and take a license to use ...'.

This beautifully written record is accompanied by an equally detailed map, to the scale of 3 chains to 1 inch, showing the Darkhill furnaces. The pipes referred to are shown in red, running from the spring to the Smith's shop.

Local residents relate how, as children, their first task after coming home from Ellwood School, was to get fresh water from this spring. Still today, even in the driest summers it never dries up, which was doubly important then when water mains were unknown. The 19th century population Census shows that many people lived hereabouts. Bracken now covers what little remains of their homes.

Below the tramroad, near the spring, is a semi-circular retaining wall holding back the bank. Here, under a protective layer of earth, is a radial brick floor where a kiln stood. After excavation and recording in the 1970s, areas vulnerable to frost damage were covered to preserve them.

In the upper part of the site, before a descent in level, lies the cradle of where modern complex steel alloys evolved. Contained within a curved retaining wall is another, slightly smaller, sunken circular area with a radiating pattern brick floor that shows severe heat damage. It too is hidden beneath a protective layer of earth.

Here stood a smaller kiln that was ideal for experimental work. Beside it are the sites of four ovens or furnaces, suitable to take crucibles. Behind, at a slightly higher level, is a large Smith's shop. Here too the floor is covered with earth for preservation.

The long room adjacent was part of a self contained Brickworks (built pre 1818). Much later, it became a Colour Works. An odd reference to Dark Hill furnace, which serves to illustrate its mystery, appears in a ledger with the grand title of *The Original Directory to the Royal Forest of Dean 1870*. The book is a diary kept by James Thompson, aged 18, who was born at Lords Hill House, Coleford. Entry 505 states, in clear copperplate handwriting:

'Dark Hill Furnaces are not worked at present. There is a large pond of water, one on one side and also one on the lower side. Blacksmiths are employed in some parts to make hammers. There is a most beautiful spring of well water which is useful. Some parts of it was used for a fight between the Liberals and the Blues, namely Kingscot and Marlin and old Blue Somerset, he lost a grand day that time.'

It is not known what exactly the nature of the 'fight' between the Liberals and the Blues was. The Smithy and the two large

Blacksmith's hearths, just beyond the small kiln and ovens, are more extensive than needed to make only hammers but ideal for working new metals to discover their properties. Robert Mushet carried out much of his secret experi-mental work in one of the out buildings at his home, Tump House, at Cinder Hill in Coleford. He mostly worked alone but when he needed help, he and his wife worked as one. She pumped the bellows and held the red-hot billets in tongs while Robert hammered them into shape. They fought the problems as a team.

Robert and his wife working as a team at the anvil.

When experiments needed scaling up, they were done at the furnaces by the Smithy. A 'Bear' lies hidden in the grass. This is the site of the small experimental 'R. Mushet & Co. Forest Steel Works' which was started in September 1847. Where better to hide a secret than adjacent to a brickworks. Lessons learned here were put into practice when the Titanic Steel & Iron Co. Ltd Works was built in 1862. Even after Titanic was in use, Robert would return here to explore other avenues of steel making, looking for special qualities.

There is another circular area, part way along the tramroad, on its southern side, below the level of the track. Clay for brick making, dug nearby, would have been brought, and tipped here. Just beyond the circular area, to the right, are the foundations of a square room. Under another protective layer of earth are brick pillars that enabled heat to circulate under a drying room floor.

Nearby is a large edge runner millstone lying on its side. It would have stood upright and would have been rotated round a trough by a pony harnessed to a beam. It was used to crush dry clay to a powder. Its edge has been re-cut but there is no sign of its re-use.

Just past the clay storing area there are more tramroad blocks crossing the track. Another loop of single-holed blocks runs alongside, now hidden under the turf verge, near a pylon.

The house 'Marefold', which was built circa 1780 (and is today the author's residence) stands in its own grounds. The term 'Marefold' describes a special place where a mare would choose to have her foal in safety. Its front boundary wall has foundry clinker decorating the top. A square hole, near the gateway, permitted the household ducks to waddle, in single file, down to the nearby pond. Some 150 years ago a family named Powell lived here and, as the following newspaper extracts show, became the unfortunate victims of a dreadful accident at the Darkhill Works:

GLOUCESTER JOURNAL, 1st August 1846
'Frightful and fatal explosion. We deeply regret to state that a steam engine at the ironworks of D. Mushet Esq. at Darkhill, near Coleford, exploded on Tuesday last, causing most frightful injuries and several deaths. A man named George Powell, and an infant also named Powell, were killed instantaneously. The child was at the time in the arms of its mother, who had arrived at the works with her husband's breakfast. No less than ten men were injured in the explosion, of whom 3 have since died,

making, as we have heard, 5 deaths altogether. An inquest was to have been heard yesterday on the bodies, before J.G. Ball Esq., Coroner; but we have not heard any further particulars of this lamentable event.'

GLOUCESTER JOURNAL, 8th August 1846

'The fatal explosion at Coleford. G.J. Ball Esq., held an inquest yesterday (Friday) week, on the bodies of George Powell, aged 26, Herbert Powell, aged 1 year and 10 months, and William Powell, aged 31, the father of Herbert, who were killed by the explosion of a steam boiler at the Dark Hill Iron Furnace, near Parkend, the property of Messrs. Mushet, which unhappy occurrence we briefly reported last week. Powell's wife and another of his children and some other persons, were dreadfully injured but expected to recover. The boiler was an old special one, but considered quite safe, and it is feared the unhappy workmen brought on the accident by negligence. According to calculations made by Mr. Walkinshaw, the engineer, he arrived at the conclusion that a force equal to 4260 tons or 9,542,400 lbs. would be requisite to have torn up the boiler, as it appeared to have been done by one effort. This would give a pressure of 656 lbs. per (sq.) inch, far beyond any ever attempted, except with Mr. Perkin's steam gun. The whole of the upper part of the boiler had been torn from the bottom near the junction, and although weighing about 3 tons, was projected into the air perpendicularly, to a height of many feet, some of the witnesses believing at least two to three hundred; it came down precisely upside down on the very spot from whence it had been torn. A verdict of accidental death was given.'

It was a terrible coincidence that the explosion occurred when Ann Powell (aged only 19 at the time) visited the site with her children. The force capable of driving a three ton boiler a hundred metres into the air would also turn brickwork, fire irons, shovels, and even the coal to feed the boiler into lethal projectiles hurled into the bodies of those gathered nearby.

The horrendous mayhem and carnage caused by the explosion needs little imagination. The incident dramatically reminds us of the harsh reality of the lot of the working man at that time. There was no welfare state to look after them. Was Ann left disfigured

An example of a Haystack boiler. This one is now preserved at the Museum of Iron, Ironbridge, Shropshire, part of the Ironbridge Gorge Trust's complex.

A Haystack boiler in situ, supplying a Heslop engine at a colliery in the Middle Wood area of Shropshire.

and what was the psychological impact of her son being killed in her arms? What disabilities did the other child have to live with as he grew up or did he die later because of the accident? The 1851 Census is unclear. The number of deaths given in an account of the accident is higher. It may include those who died subsequently.

The only other historical note we have of Ann, besides the Population Census, is an entry in *The Register of Cow Keepers, Dairymen and Purveyors of Milk*, for the West Dean Rural District Council, in an entry for 14th February 1887: '*Ann Powell of Marefold is registered as a Cow Keeper and Purveyor of Milk*'.

She would have toured the local houses on the Knoll with a pony and trap. Ladling the fresh milk from a churn into the householders' own jug or pitcher. The only means of keeping the milk from going sour was to keep it covered over in as cool a spot as could be found.

Down the slope in front of 'Marefold''s gate, under an oak tree, is a glimpse of a stone arch. This is the entrance to a coal mine owned by the Mushets. Freeminers must not mine under graveyards or orchards and 'Marefold' was safely protected by its orchard. The mine was unsuccessful. Over the small ford, known locally as 'the splash', the kilns of Milkwall Brickworks stood and beyond are the remains of the Titanic Steelworks.

In the area to the front of 'Marefold', clay was dug for brick making. There are rumours that there was a Clay Mine here but there is no record of it on the mining maps of the area, kept in the Deputy Gaveller's Office at Forest Enterprise, Bank House, in Coleford.

Nearby there are stone lined culverts and leats hidden away amongst the undergrowth that would have drained the coal level above. A great amount of clay must have come out when they were dug and thus the story of a clay mine could have originated, for the spoil would not have been wasted. It would have been used for making bricks.

You can imagine a fellow Forester asking "*Wat yea diggin me old Butt? A cley mine?*" Or it may be just a tale to confuse any 'vurriners' ('Foreigners') daft enough to ask. Anyone from outside the Forest is thought of as a 'Foreigner'– even if they may have lived in the Forest for 40 years.

Such tales are born out of Foresters great sense of humour and kindly hearts, which counterbalanced their harsh living standards when part of the close knit communities of coal miners and their families. The threat of tragedy was always in the offing when least expected.

Subsequent excavation obliterated the route of the tramroad. It had run across to 'Steel Works Cottage', which had been the office of the Titanic Steelworks. The end of the cottage building is cut back to enable the track to run round it. The tramroad continued to Milkwall, crossing the subsequent railway line via a swing bridge. The remains of the stone abutment is still there.

Other mines and quarries on Gorsty Knoll have been worked within living memory. A resident tells of her childhood memories of the 'white' (grey) pony that pulled the tubs. As the miners dug further the rope got longer. The pony had to walk further down the slope before the tub, full of coal, appeared. Nearby lie slag tips of the Titanic Steelworks and the foundations of a pump house which sent water up to the works.

Large buttressed walls of the upper level stand silently over the lower levels of the Ironworks today. The quiet Aaron's Pond, where Aaron Hart, a haulier, had a licence to water his horses at the turn of the 20th century, is an ideal place to contemplate the hive of activity that was once here.

If there are white vapour trails high in the sky from passing aircraft, remember they might not be there but for what happened on Gorsty Knoll in the Forest of Dean. The technical and economic world moves remorselessly on. It is inevitable that someone else would have made the discoveries. Many claim that distinction but Robert Mushet deserves his place on any relevant Roll of Honour.

The Darkhill Ironworks site is of both national and international importance. Robert was born into the world of wood and iron. He went on to raise the curtain on the world stage of the age of steel alloys. Darkhill is where the score was written. Here the rehearsals were held and the prelude was performed.

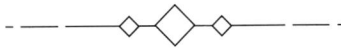

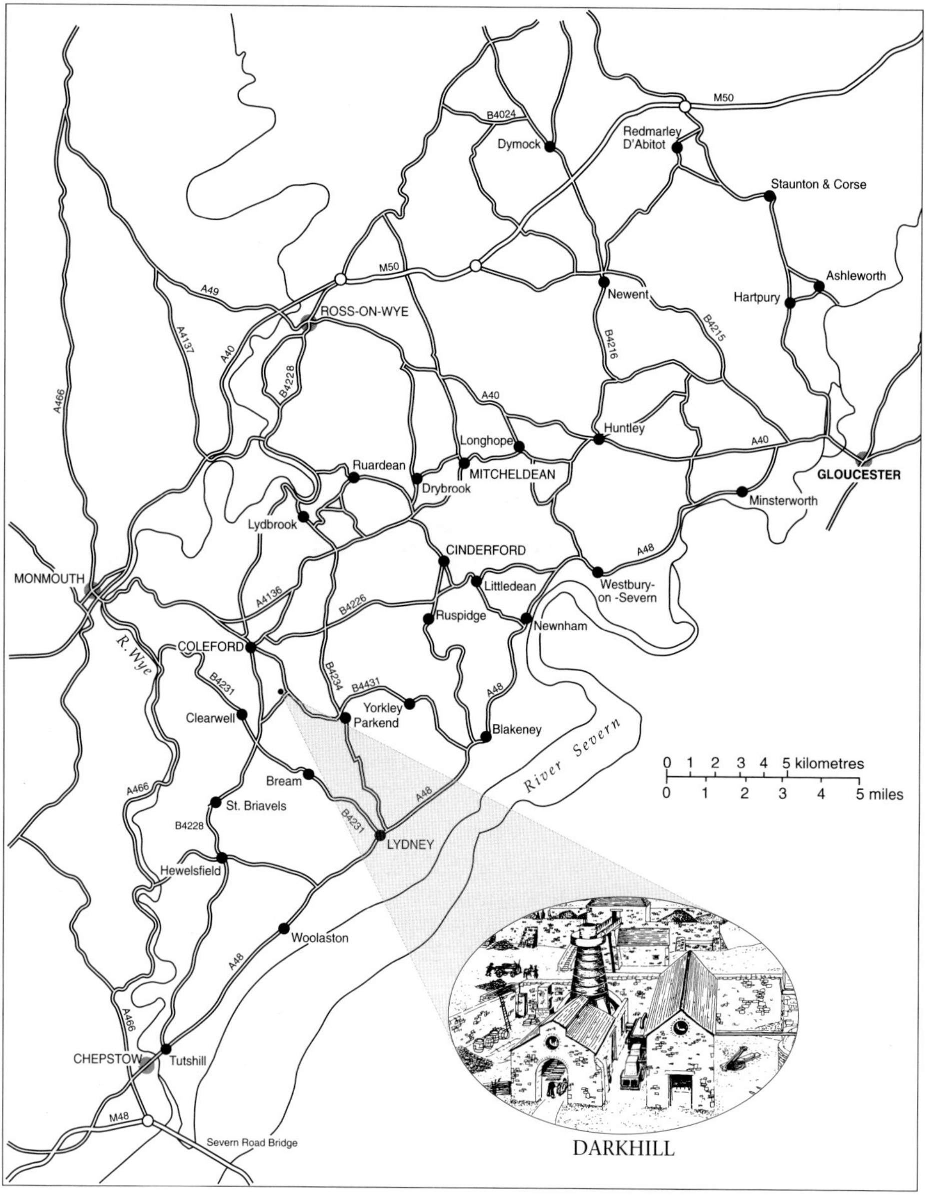

M50
B4024
Dymock
Redmarley D'Abitot
Staunton & Corse
Ashleworth
Hartpury
M50
A49
ROSS-ON-WYE
Newent
B4215
B4216
A4137
A40
B4228
A466
A40
Longhope
Huntley
A40
Ruardean
MITCHELDEAN
GLOUCESTER
Drybrook
Minsterworth
Lydbrook
CINDERFORD
A48
MONMOUTH
Littledean
Westbury-on-Severn
A4136
B4226
Ruspidge
Newnham
R. Wye
COLEFORD
B4231
B4234
B4431
A48
Yorkley
Parkend
Clearwell
Blakeney
River Severn
0 1 2 3 4 5 kilometres
0 1 2 3 4 5 miles
Bream
A466
A48
St. Briavels
B4231
B4228
LYDNEY
Hewelsfield
Woolaston
A48
A466
CHEPSTOW
Tutshill
M48
Severn Road Bridge
DARKHILL

The location of Darkhill within the Forest of Dean.

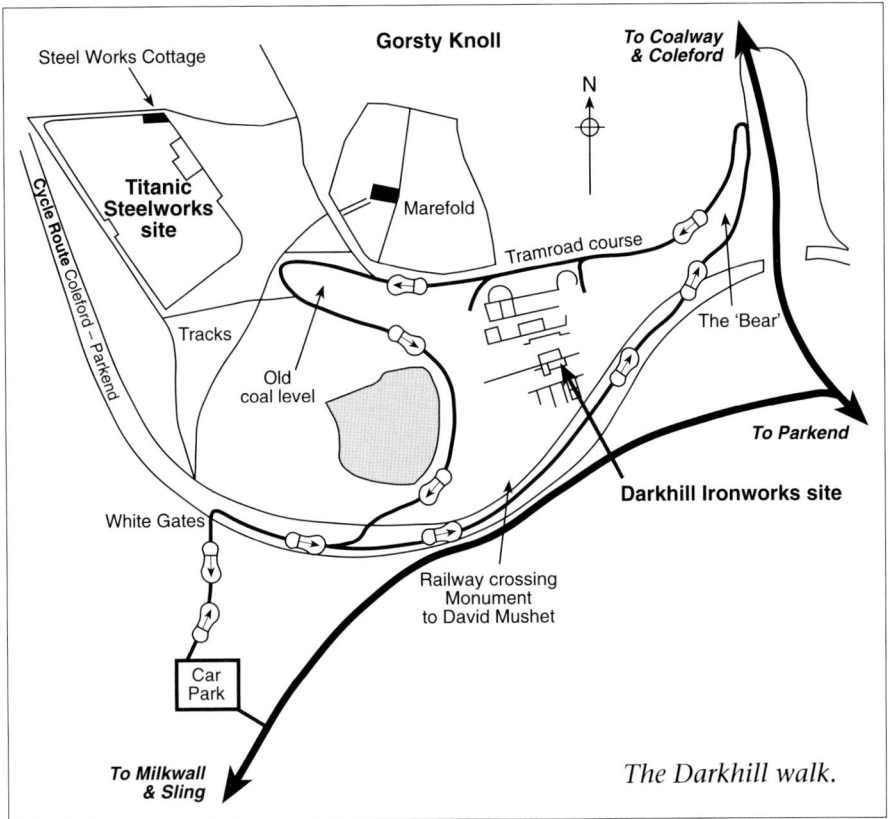

The Darkhill walk.

The ruins of the Titanic Steelworks appear on the right of this circa 1930 picture postcard. The 'White Gates' can be seen towards the centre of the scene.

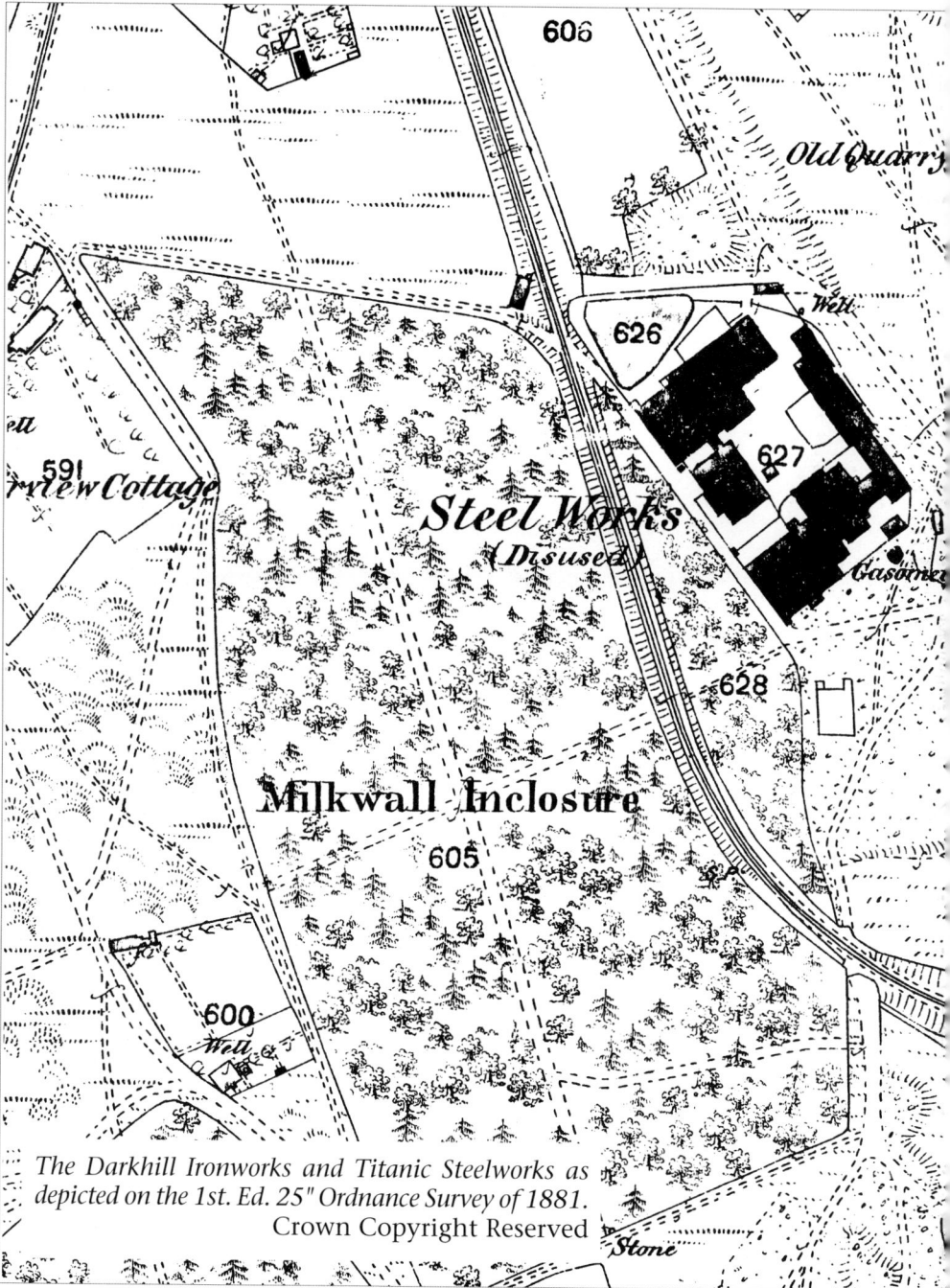

The Darkhill Ironworks and Titanic Steelworks as depicted on the 1st. Ed. 25" Ordnance Survey of 1881. Crown Copyright Reserved

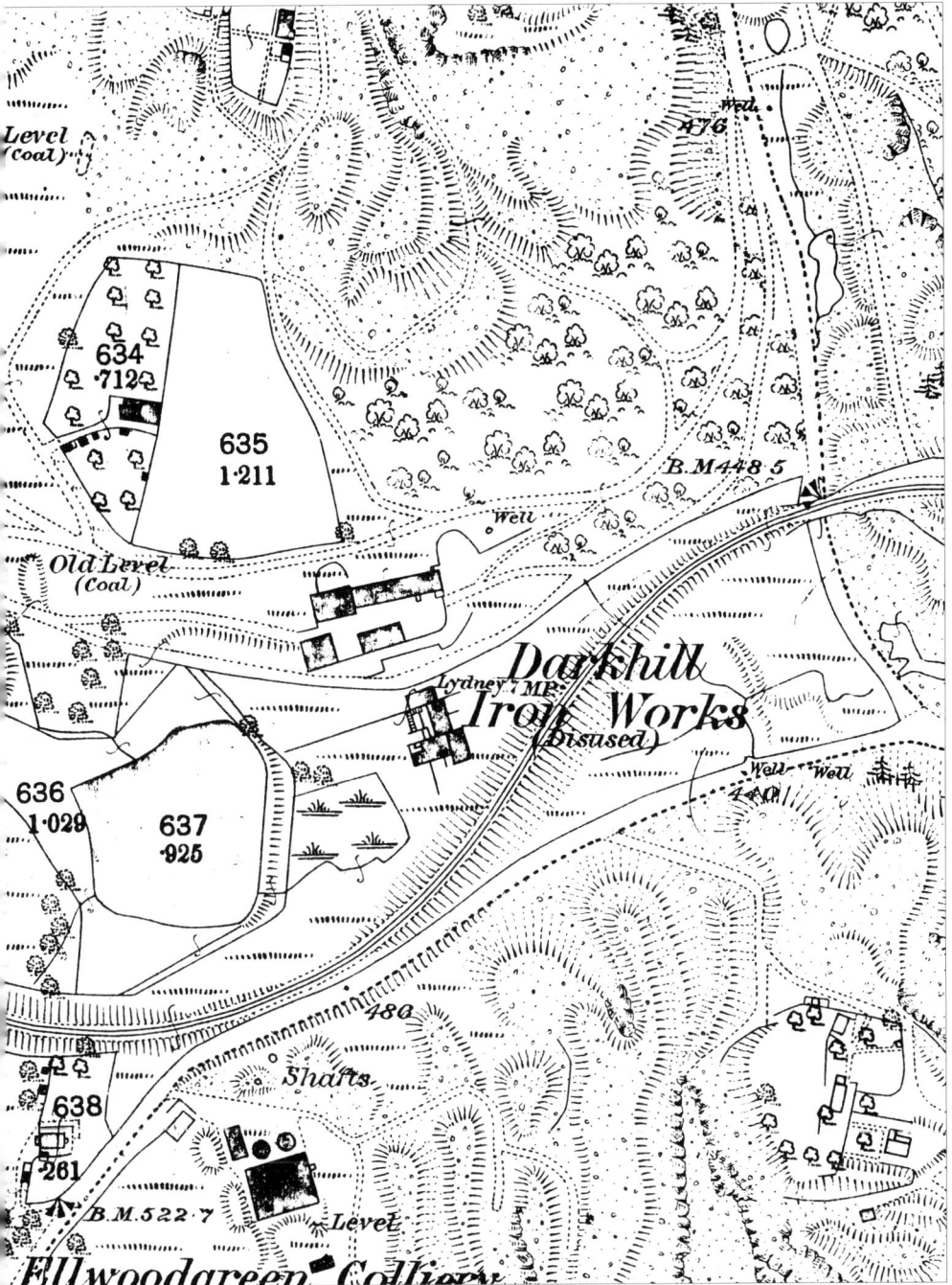

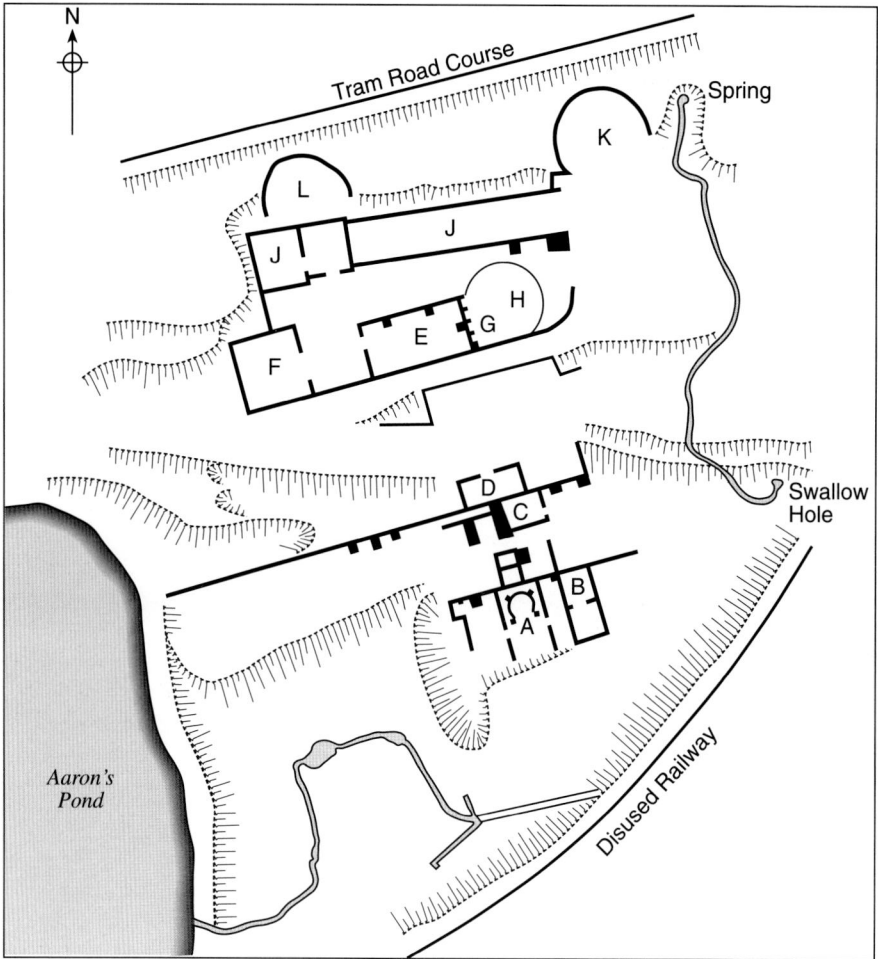

DARKHILL IRONWORKS

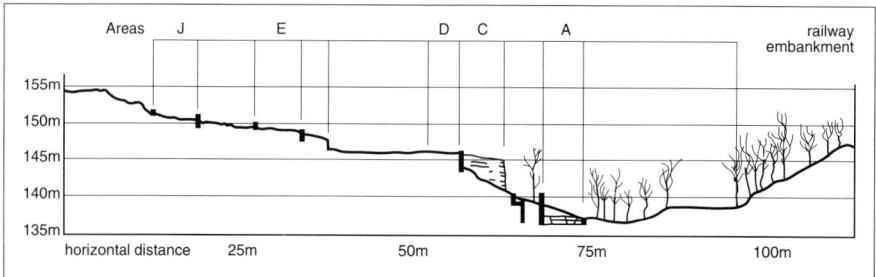

SECTION THROUGH SITE

A. Blast Furnace (Lower Terrace)

It is clear that what now remains of the blast furnace is not David Mushet's original experimental furnace of 1818/19, which was, in fact, nothing more than a cupola. It is known that the experimental or cupola furnace had an internal volume of about 1000 cubic feet (28 cubic metres). By 1845 it was 'much worn and wasted'. *Volumetric capacities of blast furnaces for the years before circa 1840 are hard to find but it is reasonable to assume that such a furnace would be of not less than about three times the volume of the experimental one. So it would be an orthodox blast furnace of the period, which was the commercial basis of Darkhill. The furnace, of which some small remains still exist, is of much later date. In 1845, during the short-lived partnership of the Mushet brothers, £1000 was spent on enlarging and improving the furnace, whilst in 1846 hot-blast apparatus was added. David Mushet junior records that he built the furnace* 'upon the principles of Mr J Gibbons', *who was the pioneer of the circular hearth, which he introduced in 1832. It was so successful that it was soon adopted widely. What little now remains of the furnace itself shows quite clearly that the hearth was circular, so the ruins are definitely of the final period of operation. There were plans for improvements but not all were carried out. The whole area has been surveyed and mapped. Every detail has been recorded and sectional drawings made. The* 'Horseshoe' *Hearth now lies under a protective layer of earth as does much of the surrounding area. The* 'heals' *of spring arches in the stonework in this area leave us with more questions than answers. It was a period of rapid change and advancement. In the period prior to this part of the site being abandoned, it was very much a case of* 'make-do and mend' *and thus alterations were not made with the care with which the original building work was done.*

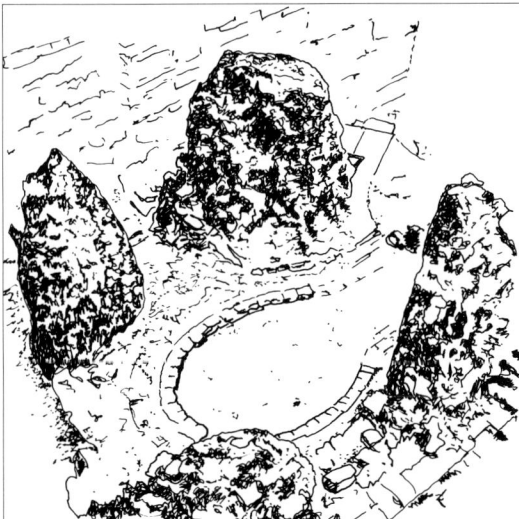

B. Blowing Engine (Lower Terrace)

When looking at the furnace area from the south, the engine house is located to the right. An inventory of 1845 tells us that two new boilers were installed. These were of the cylindrical, egg-ended type, 36ft long and 4ft diameter (10.9 x 1.2m). The inventory shows that the furnace was blown by a steam engine with a steam cylinder 24 in. in diameter on the railway embankment side and a blowing cylinder 60in in diameter (0.6 x 1.5m) on the north side of the dividing wall in the Engine House. There is no information on whether it was a wooden or a cast iron rocking beam. The inventory records that the old cupola furnace was still on site. In addition there were 'A casting house, a water regulator, a bridge or filling loft, an office and a round boiler'. *There is no trace of the casting house, which would have abutted on the furnace to the south. Nor has anything been found, as yet, of the regulator. This was a device which was popular in the first half of the 19th century to even out the fluctuations in the blast caused by a reciprocating blowing engine. Regulators were of various types but the one at Darkhill was a water regulator. It was an enclosed cistern, containing water, into which the blast was passed before it went to the tuyeres. It should have been as close as possible to the blowing engine and furnace. At Darkhill, it might have been in the un-named enclosure shown on the plan behind the furnace and below the Lower Foundry building but so far there is nothing to show that it was. The regulator might have been made of wrought iron plates, like a boiler, in which case it would probably be impossible to find*

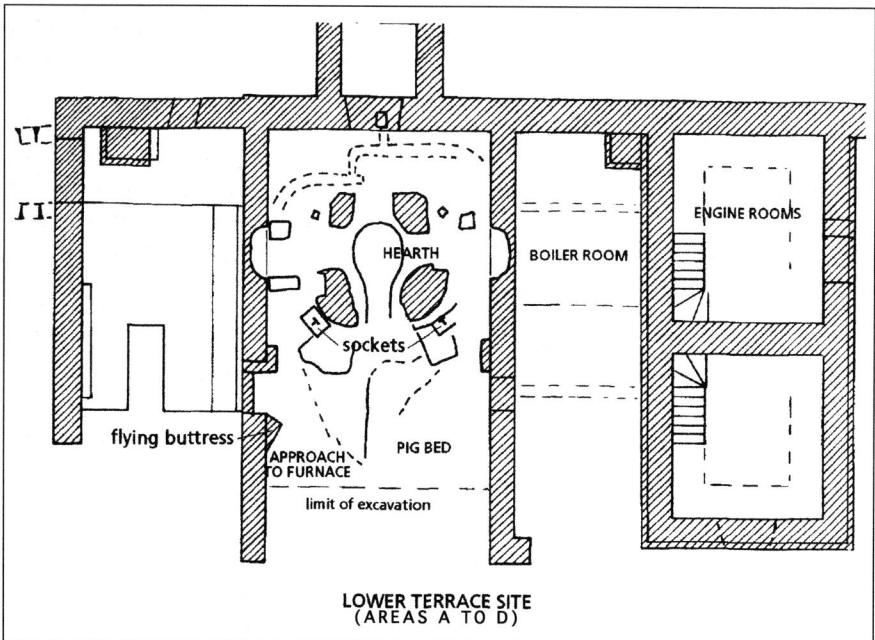

LOWER TERRACE SITE
(AREAS A TO D)

any traces of it. The building was probably partly demolished when the blowing engine was removed, either for its scrap value or for re-use elsewhere but no records exist. It may have been a case of a 'free-for-all' to re-use the stone when the railway embankment buried some of the partly demolished buildings.

C. Charging Incline (Lower Terrace)

The 'Middle Terrace Foundry buildings' above the Blast Furnace, Area 'A', may be the filling house. A stone-built bridge abutment leads from it towards the furnace top but the top of the later retort was higher and thus a walkway, supported on the incline, may have been the solution. The intervening space would have been spanned by a wooden or cast iron bridge. It must be remembered that anything made of metal would have been subsequently taken for scrap and wood collected for fires. Over the years the incline has suffered the ravages of weather and time. Considerable effort has been made to stabilise and partially restore it to give some idea of its size.

D. Charging Preparation Area or Charging Room (Middle Terrace)

An area above the furnace was required for accurately weighing out the raw materials for making the iron to the quality that was required for malleable tin plate making, as developed by Robert Mushet's father, David. He made iron here for twenty years and amassed a fortune. Raw materials would have been measured by the barrow load coming in but the Crucible process required far more accurate measurements. The land adjacent to the Charging Preparation Room is where these raw materials – iron, coke and lime – would have been stored. There would have been fumes and smoke everywhere when the coke was being made.

E. Smith's Shop (Upper Terrace)

The Smith's shop is far too big to have been the normal maintenance smithy which every blast furnace had, for repairing and making tools and ironwork. The building was marked 'Smiths shop' on a plan of 1866 and this has been accepted uncritically. The 1878 25in OS calls the building a 'Smithy' but it is also marked, on a plan which is unfortunately undated, as 'Mr Mushet's Brickyard and Buildings'. There are three stone and brick bases, of what would have been smiths' hearths, remaining. In front of each is a stone block, let into the floor in the proper position to take the slice of a tree trunk on which an anvil was always set. This was clearly a smithy, though again it was too large to be used simply for maintenance purposes at a single blast furnace. There is evidence that hammers were made in this area which has been called the 'Upper Foundry' by local people.

F. The Edge Running Stone (Upper Terrace)

The 'Pounding Room', as it has been designated, contains a large round flat stone 78 inches in diameter by 14in thick (1,981 x 355mm) lying on its side, and a number of cut stone pieces. It is an edge-runner mill stone, the cut stones being the foundation for the vertical shaft about which the edge-runner rotated. The hole into which the shaft fitted is still there; its upper bearing would have been in the beams of the roof, which has disappeared. Power for turning the mill could have been provided by a horse or by a steam engine. There is, as yet, no trace of the latter but this is not surprising. If made of metal it would not have needed very big foundations and would itself have been a saleable object for scrap or re-use. Water power was not used here or anywhere else on the site. The mill stone is made of Pennant Sandstone. Its crushing surface has been re-cut but there is no sign of its subsequent use after its re-dressing. An edge-runner mill was used by Robert Mushet for preparing alloy powders and David probably had such a mill in his experimental barn at Coleford. The possibility exists that the mill at Darkhill was used for alloy powder preparation at one time and for brick clay at other times.

G.Furnaces and Teeming Bay, used in experiments of Crucible steel making (Upper Terrace)

The east wall of the forge is displaced by a series of small furnaces, which face east. The floor level in this area is lower than that in the forge and the back walls of the furnaces are a brick revetment supporting the high level of the forge floor. Piers projecting from the revetment wall divide it into booths. Each booth has a shallow arch above it and, at about 60 cm above its ground level, iron girders formed a bench across it. Above the remains of the benches the bricks of the structure are vitrified but the chimneys from these furnaces are not evident. It is here that most of Robert Mushet's experiments were carried out for subsequent exploitation, initially at the Titanic Steelworks and then at Sheffield. As everything done here was of a temporary nature, no account was taken of the damage caused by the extreme heat experienced all around this area. The term 'furnace' causes great confusion; when used today, the meaning is totally different to what was thought of as a furnace in the 19th century. Crucible steel making is a refining process. An area was required for accurately weighing out the raw materials for making steel by this process. One would imagine Robert Mushet would have used scales similar to those seen at the Abbeydale Industrial Hamlet, Sheffield. A coal fire would first be lit in the Crucible steel furnace. The 'pots', as crucibles were known, would be banked up with coke as the main fuel. Charges of the required amounts of raw materials would be tipped carefully through an iron funnel, a little at a time, into the heated crucible in the furnace. Care would be taken to ensure the sudden difference in temperature between that of the crucible and the raw materials was not so great as to shatter it. A lid was placed on the pot and the cover of the furnace lowered. This forced the draught through the fuel and up a chimney. The temperature required to melt steel would be about 1,550 degrees centigrade. To protect himself from the heat, Robert Mushet would have worn both a leather apron and water soaked sacking from the waist down. Most melts would take from three to four hours. The pots would then be pulled out of the furnace with long handled tongs. The scene at Darkhill and Titanic would be very similar to that at Abbeydale, where they specialised in the manufacture of scythes. Although Robert Mushet never visited Sheffield, the tools, the setting and ambience would have made him feel at home there. Today he would be surprised that common place items with which he would have been familiar now take pride of place in what would have been an everyday setting in his experience. The molten metal was poured into a mould to form an ingot in an area known as the 'Teeming Bay'. Most of the slag was skimmed off the top of the metal with the aid of a 'mop' – usually an iron bar. The pot was then gripped with a pair of round-headed tongs and the molten metal would be poured into the mould. It required great skill to be able to pour the metal straight from the crucible to the bottom of the mould without splashing the sides – the only way to produce a clean ingot without flaws. When the mould was nearly full, the fireclay 'dozzle', invented by Robert Mushet, would be placed on the top of the mould and filled with more molten steel. This provided a reservoir of metal which fed down the centre of the ingot, thus preventing what was known as 'piping' or the formation of cavities. After cooling, the 'dozzle' would be knocked off and scrapped, as this was where most of the impurities and imperfections collected. The break would show the crystal structure of the ingot, which to the trained eye would give an indication of its carbon content and thus quality. Robert Mushet worked in secrecy and it was his wife, Mary, who worked with him. While Robert man-handled the crucible with the tongs and poured the white hot molten metal into the mould, she ensured no further slag went in. Both of them would have been bathed in sweat and it demonstrates Mary's commitment to her husband and his work.

H. Kiln Base (Upper Terrace)

The floor extends east at the same level to form a round feature, with a revetment wall at its edge, and in the middle is a kiln floor. There was a circular kiln here. It was built of stone and brick, and its inner floor and walls were firebrick. The internal and external diameters of the kiln wall are 3.6m and 5.8m respectively. There are eight equi-spaced radial channels built into the floor, which penetrate horizontally through the base of the kiln wall and are filled with solid clinker. Where the channels meet the internal edge of the kiln they are 17cm wide and about 10cm deep. Around the internal edge of the kiln, short vertically set girders were discovered either side of some channels as it entered the wall. This area shows considerable signs of heat damage which could indicate subsequent temperatures far higher than that required for brick making. It too now lies under a layer of protective earth after being recorded.

J. Brick Making (Upper Terrace)

At the east end of the Upper Terrace there is a long room which, at its western end, has a solid floor of flagstones and cobbles. Just under halfway down the length of the room, the flags gave way to a hypocaust floor, which had channels running the rest of the length. The floor was supported on fourteen rows of bricks, each perhaps three courses high, and there were broad ledges of stone and brick alongside the north and south walls. This room was a brick-drying shed but the position of its furnace or other associated equipment is not known.

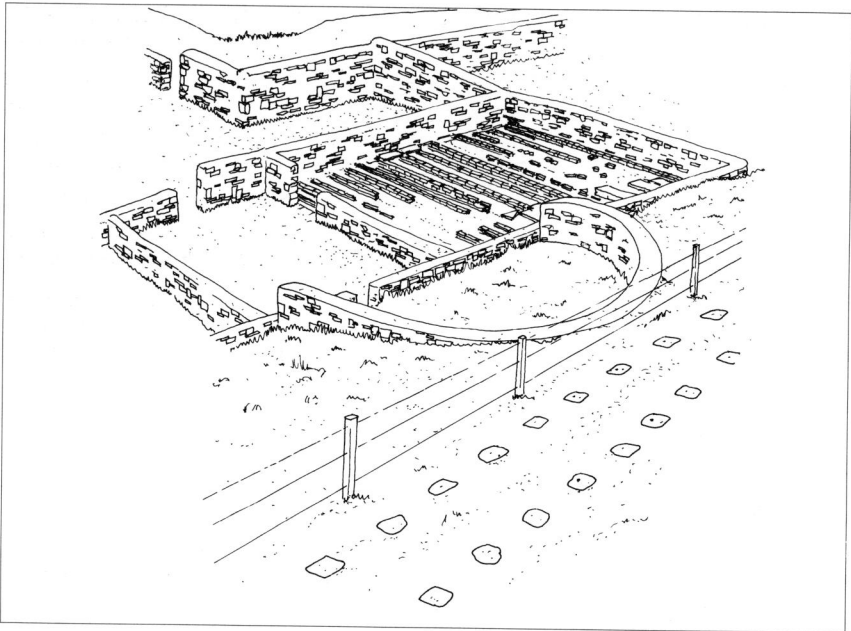

The hypocaust floor plates were not found but were possibly made of iron and would therefore have been taken away for scrap. Outside the south wall of this room, at the east end, are two buttresses which were laid against the wall after it was built, the stone work not being tied in. The only other place on the site where such heavy support was required was against a revetment wall. The middle room of this range of buildings has entrances in all of its four walls. Evidence in the east wall suggests that the doorway through it used to be at the south end, instead of in the north end where it is now. The floor in this room was laid with flagstone, most of which has been robbed. The west room of this block, like the long room, has a row of brick sided channels in it that would have supported a hypocaust brick-drying floor. The channels run south to north from an east-west conduit next to the south wall, and cease about halfway across the room. In the bottom of the east-west conduit are two brick-sided flues, which go down at least a metre below the hypocaust floor level. Presumably these flues were fed from furnaces outside the south wall of the room. The northern half of the room, where the channels cease, is completely different from the southern half and it contains the brick footings of an iron boiler or furnace. At the west side, a narrow alley with a stone and brick ridge ran by the boiler. It is thought impossible that the boiler and the brick-drying would be simultaneous activities, and it is more likely that the boiler was inserted when the brick-drying in this room had ceased.

J. Tilt Hammers (Upper Terrace)

There are reports of there being two Tilt Hammers at Darkhill and there is a similar report of them being at the Titanic Steelworks; it might well be the same Hammers having been re-located. The two buttresses along the outside of the wall of the long brick making room, Area 'J', are cited as being there to support the weight of such equipment. What the motive power was is speculation. It might have been a single cylinder horizontal steam engine of some power to drive Tilt Hammers. They could have been operated by a series of iron cogs set in iron collars on the main shafts. The main shaft would have been driven through a spur wheel and pinion, fixed to the end of the driving engine and main shaft respectively. The teeth of the spur wheel were most probably made of oak. Some Tilt Hammers could give six blows a second. The noise would have been deafening. The Tilt Hammers at Abbeydale give a good indication of size and proportions. This room was used for a variety of purposes at different times throughout its occupation.

K. Kiln Base (Upper Terrace)

In a similar revetted cutting, driven into the tramroad embankment beyond the end of the Brickworks Drying Rooms, is a radial brick floor. On this was a Haystack Brick Kiln for firing bricks. The floor has internal and external diameters of 4.46m and 7.26m, is built using bricks alone and has ten equi-spaced radial channels but in all other respects was similar to a smaller kiln on the south side of the terrace. The floor was quite spectacular but, after a few years at the mercy of rain and frost, It was beginning to show signs of damage. It is now covered with a protective layer of earth.

L. Storage area

This semi-circular area, driven into the tramroad embankment and revetted to bear the load of the bank, is accessible from the north doorway of the middle room, where there are two steps up to it. Limited excavation in the bottom of the feature has uncovered the edges of a pair of parallel footings, 70cm apart, on the same north-south alignment as the adjacent buildings and it is possible that these supported some sort of machinery. The area would have been used as the storage area for the clay prior to the brick making process. Most of the clay would have come from clay pits nearby, a little way up the valley. There are small coal mines also nearby and a great amount of clay may have had to have been dug out to get to the coal – it too would have gone to make bricks. Before they reached the coal level, many miners jested they were 'digging a clay mine', as local tradition relates.

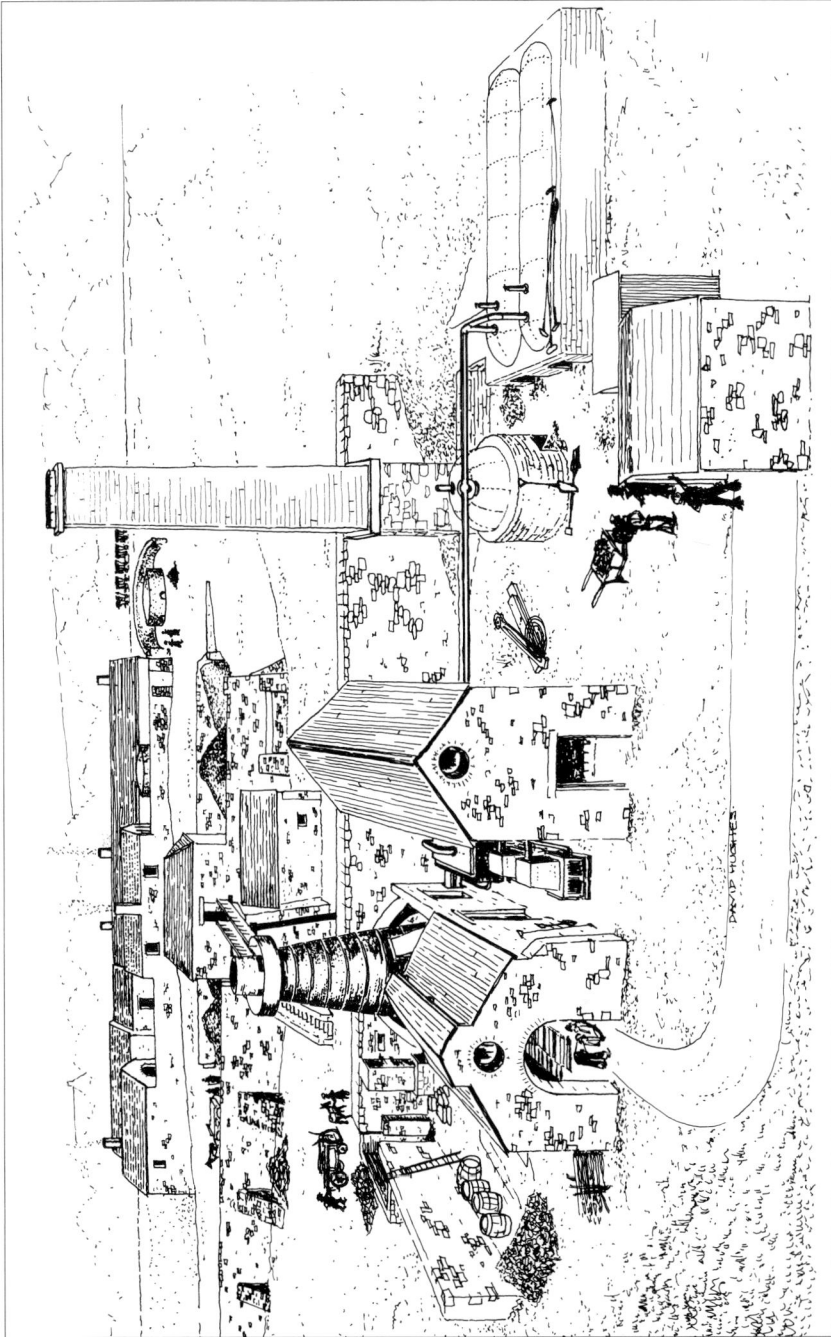

Drawing of Darkhill Ironworks as it probably appeared in 1845, showing the newly installed 'egg' shaped air reservoirs and the old haystack boiler which exploded with tragic consequences in 1846.

A model, by Alec Pope, of the lower area of Darkhill Ironworks as it would have appeared about 1854. The Haystack boiler which was the subject of the fatal accident is beside the chimney stack and the new air reservoirs are beside it. The furnace and charging bridge can be clearly seen (Area 'A' on map), the stone charging bridge having been abandoned by this date. The Mixing Shed is on the Middle level.

A view of the repaired Charging Bridge. The repairs were deliberately left without mortar showing, so as to distinguish them from the original work but this left the stonework weakened. As this 1984 picture shows, the fabric was soon in need of further repair.

A general view of Area 'A' at Darkhill in 1984, showing that the site was slipping into disrepair again since the repairs of 1978-79.

The ramparts of the Middle Terrace which, from below, look like a medieval castle.

All that needs protecting now lies beneath a covering of grass. The walls are in good repair but nature will continue to take its toll. Under present day Health & Safety requirements, the whole site has been fenced off, causing much resentment amongst those who enjoyed wandering through the ruins. However, on the plus side, damage caused by humans has been drastically reduced as a consequence.

Area 'A'. The aperture through which it is thought a pipe ran from the Blowing Engine, beyond, to the Furnace. The sunlight caught by the camera's lens lends the picture an ethereal quality which sums up the mystery of Darkhill. The site is said to stand on a Ley Line – a mystery in itself.

Area 'A'. The Horseshoe Hearth shortly after the whole area had been excavated in 1979, showing the 'teeth' made of slag.

Another angle on the Horseshoe Hearth. This all now lies under a protective layer of earth.

A panoramic view of the lower level in 1979, again showing the Horseshoe Hearth.

Looking across the Lower Terrace walls. Restoration was in hand in 1979. To the left can be seen the previously curved arch which has been altered by misguided restorers.

A picture of the Darkhill site taken shortly after excavations were finished in 1979. From top to bottom, it shows the Upper Terrace, the Middle Terrace, the Charging Bridge and the Lower Terrace, where the main Furnace stood. The excavation of the site and its restoration had been a mammoth undertaking, promoted and funded by the Forest of Dean Rotary Club and undertaken by the Manpower Services Commission. Many local schools became involved in the work too.

Top: *The arch at the back of Area 'A' which causes so much mystery. On close examination its sides are neither at right angles nor tapered. The walls of the arch are parallel but off a few degrees to the left. The stone front edge blocks and the arch are not keyed into one another either. What was the archway for? Some claim it was used only for storage purposes. There are stone lined shafts nearby creating more questions.*

Left: *The unfired Horseshoe Hearth in the middle of Area 'A' just after it had been excavated. It is now protected by a layer of earth, after a full survey of the whole of the Lower Terrace had been made – every stone and the topography – by two independent surveyors.*

The top area of the Upper Terrace showing the Brick Works, Area 'J', and the middle Areas 'H', 'G' and 'E' – perhaps the most important part of the site, historically, for it was here that Robert Mushet is known to have carried out many of his scaled-up experiments for Self Hardening steel and its derivatives.

One of the Blacksmiths' Hearths in Area 'E'.

The Clay Grinding Stone and its five segment pivotal base lie in Area 'F'. Any metal trough in which it may have run would have been taken for scrap when the site was abandoned as a brickworks. The stone is believed to have previously been used at nearby Fetterhill but it was newly dressed before being installed at Darkhill and there is no sign of its ever having been used there.

Newly uncovered drying floor in the Brickworks, Area 'J', during the 1978 dig. It is now hidden from sight by a covering of earth.

Right: *Another view of the Brick Drying Room with its under floor heating ducts.*

Below left: *Where it is thought a Tilt Hammer once stood in Area 'J'. A small sapling has grown, with time, into a tree and this picture shows the destruction caused to a buttress by the roots as it grew in size.*

Below right: *Ruins in Area 'J' photographed c1950 by Fred Osborn. This archway into the Blacksmiths Shop no longer exists; only the steps remain.*

Area 'G'. The Smithy Shop is just beyond the Crucible Furnaces.

A closer study of the Crucible Furnaces.

Area 'K'. Two views of the radial brick floor of the Brick Kiln, which is also now covered by a protective layer of earth.

Top: The broken remnants of one of Robert Mushet's crucibles, alongside two modern examples. The coffee mug gives an idea of scale although modern crucibles come in all shapes, sizes and materials. The one in the background is new. The one on the right shows the damage that modern furnaces can inflict. The round lid and shards of Robert's are unique. He was the first person to mix Kaolin, or Cornish china clay, with ordinary fire clays in the manufacture of crucibles in which steel is fused. Before his discovery he could only put about 36lbs (16.3 kilos) in each crucible and only two pots in the melting hole of each furnace. With his new mixture he could make crucibles that would take 60lbs (27.2 kilos) and increase the number of pots to four in each melting hole. Thus at a stroke output could be increased many fold at little extra cost. His secret was betrayed to others who made great fortunes out of his invention and he was bitter that he did not get any recognition for such work.

Bottom left: A broken crucible found at Darkhill during the 1978-79 digs, which is now in safe keeping at the Dean Heritage Museum at Soudley.

Below: Parts of a broken crucible found during the digs, also in the collection of the Dean Heritage Museum.

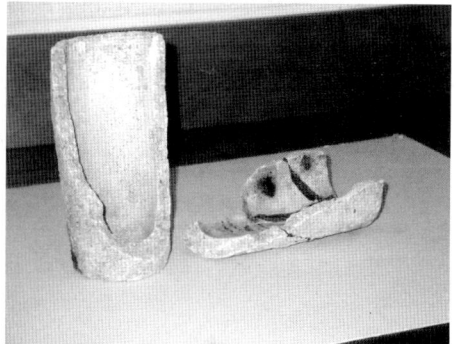

A selection of small crucibles found on site during the digs of the 1970s, now held at Soudley. The larger crucible shows signs of having been heated.

A Huntsman crucible at the Abbeydale Industrial Hamlet, Sheffield. These were used from the 1700s until about the 1930s to smelt steel. The lid is from one of Robert Mushet's crucibles – the original lid is alongside, with a modern coffee mug to give an idea of scale.

Part of a 'dozzle', another of Robert Mushet's inventions. The term has gone out of use now but these are still used when pouring molten metal into moulds. The skill is to pour the molten metal into the mould without the stream touching the sides of the 'dozzle'. The 36mm film cassette gives an idea of scale. In the collection of the Dean Heritage Museum, Soudley.

The following views were all taken at the Abbeydale Industrial Hamlet. A row of crucibles ready for heating before use. The shelves are above the fire holes of the Furnaces, against the hot flue wall. There are examples of Robert's 'dozzles' and other crucibles on the shelf, all used without payment or acknowledgement to him by the steel industry.

Moulds for making Huntsman crucibles, showing both inside and outside halves. On the floor in the foreground is a collar, used for shaping the top of the crucible when the moulds are removed.

A crucible with one of Robert Mushet's lids on top. Collars for shaping the curved top of crucibles can be seen behind, as well as other tools used. A coffee mug has again been used to give an idea of scale. Hunstman crucibles went out of use in the 1930s.

An example of a Tilt Hammer at Abbeydale. There were two of these at Darkhill, probably sited in map area 'J' and later two were used at the Titanic Steelworks – possibly the same two relocated. There is no evidence of the use of water power at Darkhill so they must have been driven by a steam engine.

The scales were used to weigh out the quantities of materials put into the crucible before it went into the furnace. Robert would have used such items over and over again. Time after time he would measure out the various ingredients and their proportions, for yet another batch of experiments as he tried to perfect the steel he was producing.

The hidden 'Bear' – a solidified mass of impurities skimmed off the molten metal before it was tapped. It is to be found further along and just to the left of the cycle track which runs past the Darkhill site, opposite the traffic sign on the road below.

The author's dog 'Tammy' stands in the little water left at what was an important supply for local people and the subject of 'An Indenture made in 1866 on the 17th day of October', *against Robert Mushet, who had overlooked taking out a licence for a pipe drawing water off this spring to the Blacksmith's Shop. Today, it still never runs dry, even in the hottest summer months.*

Samuel Osborn

S amuel Osborn was born in Ecclesfield near Sheffield in 1826. When he was 26, having worked initially as a draper and then in the tool industry, he went into business for himself making hand-made files. Through hard work, he prospered and his meeting with Robert Mushet ensured Sheffield became an unchallenged machine tool steel centre for the next hundred years. He was much respected and had a reputation for looking after his workers.

Robert Mushet met Samuel Osborn in 1870 and it was a case of a meeting of minds. Osborn understood the significance and importance of Mushet's work. He received the rights to manufacture all Robert's steels, including the sole right to make the new wonder material 'Mushet Special Steel'. In return, Robert hoped he had obtained the financial security he most wanted, which would come from the ensuing royalties.

Unfortunately Osborn, although made a Master Cutler in 1873, was forced into liquidation in 1874. However, Robert's sons Henry and Edward had gone to work for Osborn in Sheffield, and they strove to continue the business and improve the product.

The newer versions of Mushet's steel conquered the world. The Franco-Prussian War and the war in the Crimea ensured future success, at the peak of which, Osborns of Sheffield monopolised world machine tool steel production. Samuel Osborn became Mayor of Sheffield in 1891 and died while in office.

Samuel Osborn JP.

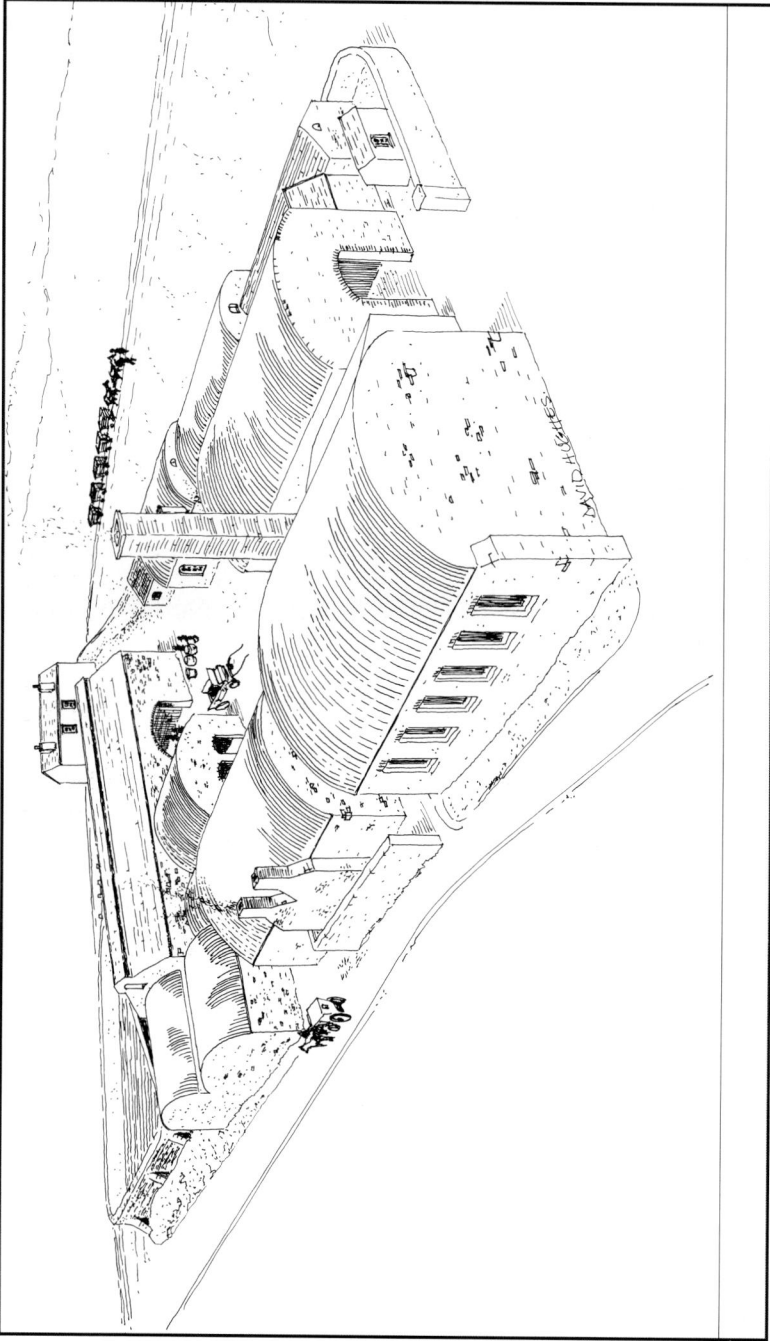

Drawing recreating the Titanic Steelworks, circa 1865. It was done using what clues could be found from the 1878 25 in. OS and photographs of the ruins in later years. The Milkwall-Parkend tramroad ran along the rear of the site, the corner of the Office being cut off to accommodate its route.

The Titanic Steelworks

When Robert's experiments produced what he called 'Titanic Cast Steel', he was for once euphoric. He had endured years of poverty and he felt that the potential for this new product would be tremendous and that it would be in great demand throughout the growing industrial world. The old works would just not be able to cope.

One of the new steels on which he pinned his hopes was the first to use Titanium in its manufacture and because of this Robert decided to name his new operation The Titanic Steelworks, trading under the title The Titanic Steelworks & Iron Works Co. Ltd. It came into existence on 22nd of October 1862 close to the old works at Darkhill, on a two-acre site slightly nearer to Coleford. Outside people and money were brought in.

For the new works there was a change in the appearance of the buildings. The majority of houses and works buildings in the Forest had, until then, been constructed with pitched or gabled tiled roofs. The new buildings had corrugated iron roofs – the latest technological development. On examination of the few photographs that still exist, it may be argued they represented the influx of the new money and ideas.

The like of it all had never been seen before in the Forest of Dean. Three hundred men were employed at the Titanic Works, with drop hammers thumping all day and the furnaces going full blast, smoke belching from their four chimneys.

Profitability, though, still eluded them and it was thought even more money was needed to solve the problem. Unfortunately, demand did not live up to expectations and, in desperation, Robert went back to his experiments, out of sight and hopefully out of mind, beside the brickworks at Darkhill. Although the apothecary's dream has always been to make gold from base metals, making steel direct from iron was a more practically obtainable one and maybe even more profitable.

With R. Mushet's Special Steel, he thought he had found his equivalent to gold. It was self hardening in air. When used for making cutting tools, they kept their cutting edge even when hot and therefore they could be put to more demanding uses, such as longer lasting and more effective mining drill bits. Lathes could have better cutting heads that did more, lasted five times longer and thus were more economic.

During the years of operation, Titanic had not led to the fortunes hoped for. Many theories are put forward as to why. The iron ore in the area was costly to mine, as the easily accessible ore had already been worked out. Imports were expensive because mass transport was almost non existent in the Forest, beyond the power of teams of horses. Even when the railways were built, they did not provide the easiest service. Location, technical and economic difficulties are all put forward, and, with some 300 men employed, was there also a case of what accountants would call over-manning?

There are stories, even related today, that materials were brought in and carried away in cider barrels, in the middle of the night, using trains of pack animals. When the railway arrived, materials were re-routed through many different agents to confuse anyone trying to learn anything! All of which must have added to the costs.

The Titanic Company was wound up in 1874 as the main centre of production was now in Sheffield. Some processing of the materials still took place at Gorsty Knoll but everything was shrouded in great mystery.

By the 1960s, the buildings had lost their roofs and what remained was considered unsafe. The last detailed photograph taken shows a pigeon loft within the walls of the extensive but crumbling buildings. The bulldozed material was used as hard-core for the approach to the Wye Bridge section of the first motorway Severn Bridge crossing at Chepstow.

A few of the smaller buildings are still there but the roofs of some have already collapsed. The one building intact is the Works Office, which Robert Mushet would have known well. There were times when he slept there while he awaited the outcome of some of his firings. It is a private residence at the time of writing. Please respect the occupier's privacy.

$$- — —◇〈〉◇— — -$$

Two photographs of the Titanic Steelworks prior to its demolition in the early 1960s. The stables are on the far right of the top view and in the right foreground of the bottom one. The Milkwall – Ellwood Road passes behind the trees in the background.

These two photographs of the remains of the Titanic Steelworks were taken on 13 May 1961 by Richard Dagley-Morris. No detailed analysis of Titanic has, as yet, been done, so the uses of the various buildings are currently not known.

A general view of the site. By this date, much of what remained was deemed unsafe and was demolished a few years later, the stone being used as hardcore in the construction of the approach to the Severn road bridge in 1966.

The Works Office seen through the window aperture of one of the outbuildings. At the time of writing English Heritage is considering scheduling both the Darkhill and Titanic Works sites. Grant Aid would safeguard these important historic sites and ensure their future interpretation and maintenance. At the present time, the Works Office is a private residence, named 'Steel Works Cottage'. The author requests that the occupier's privacy is respected at all times.

The remains of the stables and adjacent building at Titanic.

A general view of the remains of the Titanic Steelworks. The largest building, the Works Office, is now a residence and has been modified to include modern facilities.

This picture indicates that many alterations were carried out to the works over the years. The Works Office appears again in the background.

The slag heap which lies between the Darkhill and Titanic sites. It is above the level of Darkhill, so it may be assumed that the slag came from the Titanic Works.

A further selection of photographs taken at the Abbeydale Industrial Hamlet, near Sheffield. In the top views, crucible tongs, crucibles, furnace tools and irons are shown in a scene that would have been familiar to Robert Mushet, even though he never visited any other foundry and are similar to what would have been found at the Titanic Steelworks.

Furnace holes and a crucible and lid, with some 'dozzles' in the background and tools waiting to be used – typically, how a small 19th century steelworks would have looked. Although it was thirsty work, the coffee mug is only there to give an idea of scale once again.

The entrance into one of Robert's coal mines, just below 'Marefold', which unfortunately was located just under the edge of the coal seam. Some have thought it was a drain for other drift mines further up the hillside but there are other drainage tunnels for that purpose, now well hidden under thick undergrowth. This may be one of the 'famed' clay mines, that possibly being all they found. Even so, it would not have been wasted effort, the clay being used to make bricks.

Drawing of a typical Forest of Dean tramroad waggon

Reverse curve of tramroad blocks passing between 'Marefold' and Darkhill Ironworks, on the way to Parkend from Milkwall.

Remains of the tramroad, above, skirting the 'Marefold' property, on the left; Darkhill Ironworks lies below on the right. The stones were put there by Forest Enterprise to prevent further erosion by vehicular traffic. The view below shows the blocks of the main tramroad and a passing loop, looking towards Darkhill and Milkwall.

The railway pointwork monument raised in 1999 to commemorate both father and son, David and Robert Mushet, and the pioneering work they did in this small valley. The remains of Darkhill Ironworks can be seen in the background.

Robert Forester Mushet Today

There is so little in the way of contemporary sources for us to study today that will give a clearer insight into events in the 19th century, and which might provide further clues to better enable us to judge Robert Mushet's standing

We only have hindsight, born of the cynicism of our present day standards, to guide us. The knowledge of human nature has few surprises left for us today. But is our insight always accurate? There is no one alive, in this instance, to tell us but we do have the nearest to a first hand account in *The Story of the Mushets* by Fredrick Osborn JP, who died in 1950. His book was published posthumously by his brother in 1952.

In 1898 Fredrick Osborn, who worked on 'Robert Mushet Special Steel' with Henry Mushet (Robert's son), went into partnership with his brothers and in 1948 he succeeded Sir Samuel Osborn, junior, as Chairman of the board of Osborns. Thus, we have a direct link with the past. Stories of the events would have been handed down through the family by word of mouth. Although not written down, it is surprising how accurate such tales can be. One accepts that prejudices bend and twist any story as it is retold but there is always the ring of truth there too.

In fact the written word can be far more suspect and such errors get repeated again and again by unsuspecting researchers, who only read up on what has been written before. It is easy for mistakes to be perpetuated and unsuspectingly to be subsequently taken as fact. With the Internet, such errors become instantly worldwide.

If it had been available, Robert would have put the Internet to good effect. He would have used it to circulate his 'little volume', *The Bessemer Mushet Process or Manufacture of Cheap Steel*, to tell the world of his achievements.

Robert Mushet's wife, Mary Ann, was his constant companion and strength. She helped him with many of his experiments. From working the bellows, to holding the tongs while he explored the qualities of the latest batch of new steel he had made. Mary was the only one he could truly trust. She was the only witness to his many disappointments and failures. She encouraged and supported him in every way she could. She gave him the courage to go on when everyone else either doubted or derided him.

We come very close to the man in the dedication in his 'little volume':

TO HER
WHO FOR FORTY YEARS,
HAS BEEN MY TRUE AND FAITHFUL PARTNER;
IN HEALTH AND IN SICKNESS;
IN JOY AND IN SORROW;
A VIRTUOUS WOMAN;
A CROWN TO HER HUSBAND;
MORE PRECIOUS THAN RUBIES;
AN EXAMPLE TO HER FELLOW-WOMEN;
AN HONOUR TO MY KINDRED;
AND A CONSISTENT
BELIEVER IN HER LORD AND REDEEMER
JESUS CHRIST.

R. F. MUSHET.

31ˢᵗ March, 1883.

Evidently, he was a man who recognised that he was king 'in his own castle' and knew that it was his dear wife who was responsible. That drastically contrasted with how he felt he was seen by everyone else, something which made him yearn painfully for recognition from the rest of the world. Unfortunately, such status is usually only received when currying favour, which he was unable to give, or when recognition will reflect favourably on those giving it.

Robert Mushet fed from the crumbs off the rich men's table. By the middle of the 20th century, he was largely forgotten. Can we, at the beginning of a new millennium, give him the credit he deserves without detracting from others' achievements at the time? For those who want to see them, the facts are there.

If judged by his own financial success he does not qualify. If judged by the world's technological advancement and by other people's enrichment, he is truly the indisputable father of modern steel alloy production and as such, he should be respected.

The plaque on the monument to the Mushets near Darkhill.

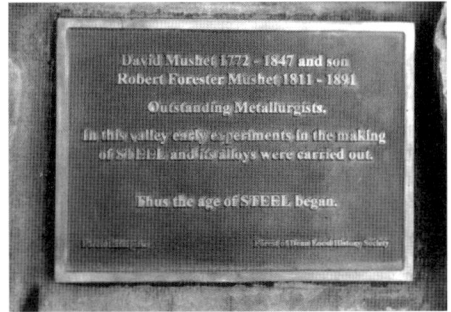

David Mushet 1772 - 1847 and son
Robert Forester Mushet 1811 - 1891

Outstanding Metallurgists.

In this valley early experiments in the making
of STEEL and its alloys were carried out.

Thus the age of STEEL began.

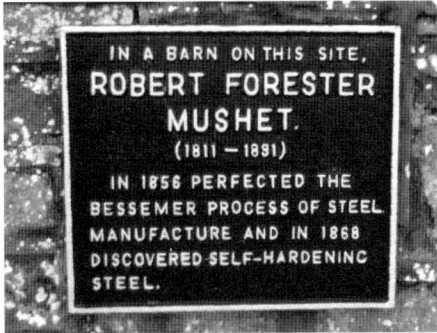

IN A BARN ON THIS SITE,
ROBERT FORESTER
MUSHET.
(1811 — 1891)

IN 1856 PERFECTED THE
BESSEMER PROCESS OF STEEL
MANUFACTURE AND IN 1868
DISCOVERED SELF-HARDENING
STEEL.

Plaque on a wall at Cinder Hill near Forest House Hotel.

Robert Mushet's legacy is to be found in steelworks the world over today. A spectacular display of sparks shoots from a Bessemer Converter which is about to have its charge of molten steel poured at a steelworks in Workington in 1973.

IN
THIS HOUSE
LIVED

DAVID MUSHET
1772 - 1847
AND HIS SON
ROBERT FORESTER MUSHET
1811 - 1891

PIONEERS
IN
IRON AND STEEL

THE FOREST OF DEAN LOCAL HISTORY SOCIETY

ERECTED BY

Plaque on the wall of Forest House Hotel, Cinder Hill, Coleford, where both Mushets lived.